GOOD HOUSEKEEPING
PRESSURE COOKERY

GOOD HOUSEKEEPING
PRESSURE COOKERY

BY

Good Housekeeping Institute

ILLUSTRATED BY

Julia Fryer

BOOK CLUB ASSOCIATES
LONDON

This edition published 1977 by
Book Club Associates
by arrangement with
Ebury Press

Reprinted 1981

Cookery consultant Margaret Coombes

Home economist Betty Hitchcock
Designer Derek Morrison
Editor Amanda Atha

Colour plates by
Bryce Attwell, Anthony Blake,
Melvin Grey, Gina Harris, Michael Leale,
Frank Apthorpe

Jacket by Philip Pace

Filmset and printed in Great Britain by
BAS Printers Limited, Over Wallop, Hampshire
and bound by
Cambridge University Press
Cambridge

CONTENTS

CONTENTS

NOTES

Quantities are for four unless otherwise stated.

Use standard eggs unless otherwise stated.

Follow either the metric or the imperial version of each recipe. Don't change half-way through as justified discrepancies do occur which could alter the end result.

A trivet has been used throughout this book when applicable. When not available follow manufacturer's instructions.

COLOUR PLATES

FOREWORD

Ways of saving time and fuel in the kitchen are all important and what better way to do both than by using a pressure cooker. If you've always thought of pressure cooking in terms of stews and soups look at the range of recipes covered in this book. It takes you right out of the realms of run of the mill meals by introducing ideas like Fresh Tomato Soup cooked in 6 minutes, Pork and Spiced Cabbage in 5 minutes, Pressed Pickled Tongue which takes only 45 minutes to cook. For entertaining we suggest dishes like Coq au Vin and Crème Brûlée showing just how versatile pressure cooking can be.

Precise timing is essential for success so all our recipes have been tested to give you the necessary instructions. Follow them and you can't go wrong. There are tables setting out times for cooking vegetables (including the unusual ones like celeriac and fennel), for pot roasting joints of meat, cooking pasta, for jam making and bottling and also a detailed explanation of how to use your pressure cooker.

The Good Housekeeping team of home economists will be pleased to answer any queries on these recipes if you write (enclosing a stamped, addressed envelope) to:

Good Housekeeping Institute
National Magazine House
72 Broadwick Street
London W1V 2BP

PRESSURE COOKERS AND HOW TO USE THEM

Why use a pressure cooker?

A pressure cooker is invaluable if you're pressed for time or money – or both. Oxtail for example, which would normally take hours in an ordinary casserole, takes just 40 minutes in the pressure cooker. You can cook a caramel custard in just five minutes. In fact you can cook most dishes in half the time or even far less and you don't have to resort to expensive cuts of meat. Cheaper ones come up just as juicy and tender because under pressure the steam is forced into the meat and this tenderises it very quickly. Added to this you can, if you wish, cook a complete meal in the cooker all at once using the 'separators', thus saving not only time and fuel but also space and washing up – a godsend for bedsits, campers and caravanners. You save precious vitamins and minerals too, because the cooking time is short, the water used is minimal. Cooking smells and condensation are kept inside the pressure cooker and out of the kitchen.

Pressure cooking helps hurry up other methods of cooking: use it in conjunction with grilling or baking, for example, by precooking, say, a meat pie filling in the cooker and finishing it with the pastry lid in the oven afterwards, or use your pressure cooker for cooking in quantity to put in the freezer and for blanching vegetables. Use it for bottling fruit. Use it for practically everything in fact. Once you *have* got used to it, you'll wonder how you ever managed without. It's a great answer to the pressure of modern life.

Take no notice of horror stories about strange hissing noises and explosions of steam. If you follow the manufacturer's instructions there's no reason why anything should go wrong. Pressure cookers made to British Standard 1746 all have built-in safety valves which are designed to release if you allow the cooker to boil dry or too much pressure to build up inside. The worst that can happen is that the sudden release of pressure gives you a bit of a jump.

Which pressure cooker should you choose?

All pressure cookers work on the same principle (see below), but there are so many different designs and sizes on the market that you may find the following guidelines useful:

1. Decide what you're going to use your pressure cooker for. If you wish to bottle fruit, make preserves or steam puddings, for example, you'll need a three pressure model. If you're only going to cook quick suppers you can make do with a one pressure one.

2. How many people are you cooking for? If you've got a large family or freezer buy a good big one. As a rough guide buy a 4·5-litre (8-pint) model for two to three people; a 5·5–7·5 litre (10–13 pint) one for four to six people. If in doubt go for a slightly larger one than you think you need. Remember that most pressure cookers mustn't be filled more than two thirds full with solid food and only half full with liquid (only models with domed lids can be filled with solid food to within 2·5–5 cm (1–2 in) of the pan rim).

3. If you're short of space, consider the design of the cooker: most models have a handle on each side to make lifting easier but some have short handles which of course take less room.

4. Cookers with non-stick linings make cleaning easier and won't stain if the water in your area is hard.

5. Check the service and guarantee offered before buying. Are replacement parts obtainable?

How it works

A pressure cooker works on the same principle as a steam engine, though the end result is delicious cooking not pistons moving. When food is cooked in an ordinary saucepan with a lid on, steam escapes and keeps the water at boiling temperature. A pressure cooker traps the steam inside the cooker and controls it. Pressure builds up inside the cooker pushing the temperature above boiling point and forcing steam into the food. This reduces the 'normal' cooking time. Pressure in the cooker is automatically maintained at the right level either by weights or by a spring and valve system. Once the required pressure is reached, only very gentle heat is needed to maintain it.

Cooking at different pressures

Some pressure cookers operate at three pressures – low (5 lb), medium (10 lb) and high (15 lb). Others have a fixed pressure of 15 lb or 7 ½ lb. Different pressures suit different processes: the higher the pressure, the quicker the cooking.

Low (5 lb) pressure is used for steamed mixtures with raising agents, to allow time for the chemical reaction to take place, and for bottling fruit, which would rise in the bottle and be overcooked at higher pressure. **Medium (10 lb)** pressure is used

for blanching vegetables for freezing and cooking fruits for jellies and jams (but not marmalade which is tougher and doesn't disintegrate as quickly and so can be cooked on high (15 lb) pressure). **High (15 lb)** pressure is used for everything else which can be pressure cooked.

Fixed high (15 lb) pressure cookers cannot be used for steamed puddings, blanching vegetables, bottling or jam making, but can be used for all the recipes in this book which indicate the use of high (15 lb) pressure.

Fixed 7 ½ lb pressure cooker. There is one type of pressure cooker on the market at the moment which has only a fixed 7 ½ lb pressure. The manufacturer's instructions should of course be followed, but the recipes in this book using high (15 lb) pressure may be cooked at 7 ½ lb pressure providing that you:

Type 1 (eg Prestige)
Type 2 (eg Tower)
Type 3 (eg Tefal)

1. Allow double the cooking time given in the recipes.
2. Double the amount of liquid indicated in the recipes.

Getting down to basics

As all pressure cookers work on the same principle, not surprisingly they are also built on the same lines. There is a saucepan base, a lid and either a pressure weight or, in the case of the fixed 7 ½ lb pressure model, a rotating valve (see below).

The base and lid Both are made of heavy aluminium or strong stainless steel. The exterior finish is either polished steel, aluminium or coloured enamel. The interior may be non-stick. The base is usually thick machined so that it can be used equally well on a gas ring, electric hotplate or solid fuel stove. The saucepan base and lid are designed to fit tightly together by locking or securing the handles.

The sealing gasket is a rubber or rubber compound ring which fits between the lid and base of the cooker to seal it firmly and prevent steam escaping. It should fit neatly between the lugs of the lid. As the gasket is made of rubber it will perish in time so be sure to check at intervals and if necessary replace it (new gaskets are obtainable from most hardware stores). If the gasket is correctly fitted and a lot of steam still escapes, this probably means you need a new one.

The steam vent is a little hole in the lid of the cooker through which steam can escape as necessary. The amount of steam released is usually controlled by the:

Pressure weight, which fits over the steam vent. This operates either at a fixed or a variable pressure, depending on the model:

Type 1 (eg Prestige) This consists of three metal rings which screw together (see diagram). The inner ring maintains a low (5 lb) pressure; the central ring screwed on to the inner one maintains a medium (10 lb) pressure and the outer ring maintains high (15 lb) pressure when the complete set is screwed together. The weight is placed on

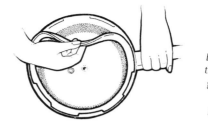

Examining the sealing gasket for signs of perishing

the steam vent once the liquid in the cooker has been brought to the boil and a steady stream of steam is coming out.

Type 2 (eg Tower) Sometimes called an 'indicator weight', this has a central black plunger marked with three silver rings. The pressure in the cooker is indicated by the number of rings visible. When high (15 lb) pressure has been reached three silver rings will show. Two rings indicate medium (10 lb) pressure and a single ring is low (5 lb) pressure. This indicator weight is placed over the steam vent *before* the contents of the cooker are brought to the boil.

The rotating valve is used instead of a pressure weight by a third type of pressure cooker (Tefal). The valve fits over the steam vent. When the correct pressure has been reached the valve starts to rotate.

The trivet is a circular platform which fits into the base of the cooker and serves either to raise food

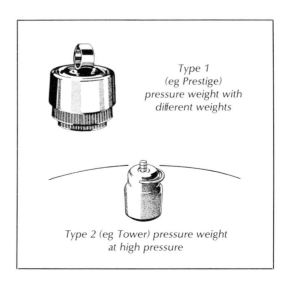

*Type 1
(eg Prestige)
pressure weight with
different weights*

*Type 2 (eg Tower) pressure weight
at high pressure*

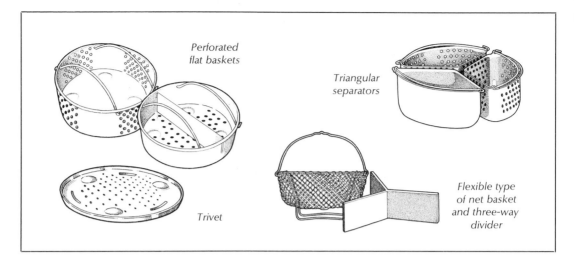

Perforated
flat baskets

Triangular
separators

Trivet

Flexible type
of net basket
and three-way
divider

above the water level for real steaming or as a means of separating dishes when more than one is being cooked at the same time.

The separators These are 'baskets' used to keep food separate during cooking, for example when cooking meat and two veg in the cooker at the same time. The design varies considerably; there are perforated flat baskets, deep triangular solid ones, deep triangular perforated ones, also a flexible type of 'net' basket.

The safety device Pressure cookers sold in this country include a safety device which releases steam fast automatically if the pressure inside the cooker builds up beyond a certain point, for example:

1. If the steam vent blocks so that steam can't escape.
2. If the cooker boils dry and therefore becomes too hot.
The device varies according to the model you are using but usually it is a rubber plug and/or metal pin in the lid which pops up to relieve the excess pressure. The pin, or centre of the plug, is generally made of a material which melts at an excessive temperature.

With normal care the safety device should never be needed. If it does come into action, however, leave the cooker to cool down com-

pletely at room temperature before attempting to put more liquid into it or trying to cool it under a tap. If the hot cooker comes into contact with cold water it may buckle. Replace the safety device once the lid is cool. To do this, either follow the manufacturer's instructions or take the cooker to a reputable hardware firm who will replace the device for you.

Step by step guide to using your pressure cooker
This is the basic method of pressure cooking but manufacturers differ slightly on points of detail so read your handbook carefully.
1. Put the trivet in the cooker if required (see page 11).
2. Pour in the liquid. The quantity of liquid is decided by the *length* of the cooking and not the amount of food to be cooked. For most models the

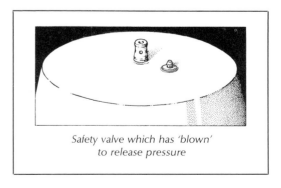

*Safety valve which has 'blown'
to release pressure*

minimum amount of liquid is 300 ml (½ pint) although some smaller models require only 150 ml (¼ pint) – check with your handbook.

3. Put the food in the cooker, following the instructions given in the recipe and making sure you don't overfill the cooker.

4. Place the lid on the cooker and fix it correctly in place. How you do this depends on which model you have.

5. Bring the cooker to pressure, according to the model you have. Proceed to cook.

6. Reduce pressure:

Types 1 and 2 (eg Prestige and Tower) Whether you do this quickly or slowly depends on what you are cooking. For some recipes a sudden drop in temperature would be disastrous. This is because if a recipe containing a volatile liquid is cooled suddenly it creates a vacuum which might whoosh out all over the place. Milk recipes may curdle. Anything with a crust such as a steamed or steak and kidney pudding may get hard and the contents burst through. Light steamed puddings tend to come out heavy. Each recipe gives precise instructions; be sure to follow them. To reduce pressure slowly: slide the cooker off the heat and allow the cooker to cool at room temperature, about 10 minutes. To reduce pressure quickly: stand the cooker in a bowl of cold water and run cold water over it until pressure has been reduced.

Type 1 (eg Prestige) Gently rattle the indicator weight with a wooden spoon or fork. When all hissing has stopped the weight can be removed easily and the lid taken off.

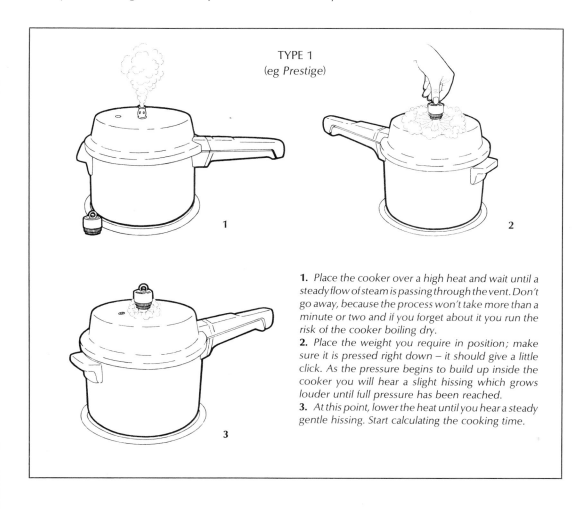

TYPE 1
(eg Prestige)

1

2

3

1. *Place the cooker over a high heat and wait until a steady flow of steam is passing through the vent. Don't go away, because the process won't take more than a minute or two and if you forget about it you run the risk of the cooker boiling dry.*

2. *Place the weight you require in position; make sure it is pressed right down – it should give a little click. As the pressure begins to build up inside the cooker you will hear a slight hissing which grows louder until full pressure has been reached.*

3. *At this point, lower the heat until you hear a steady gentle hissing. Start calculating the cooking time.*

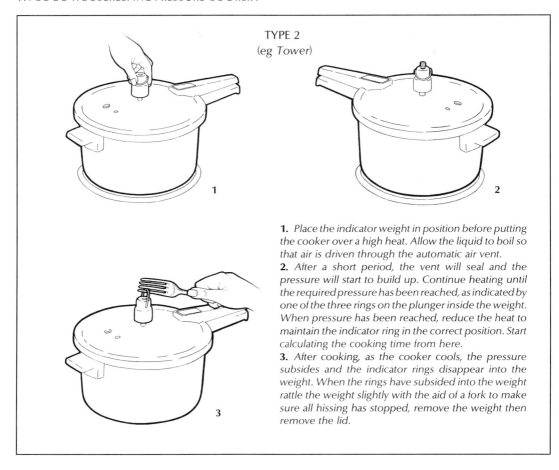

TYPE 2
(eg *Tower*)

1

2

1. *Place the indicator weight in position before putting the cooker over a high heat. Allow the liquid to boil so that air is driven through the automatic air vent.*
2. *After a short period, the vent will seal and the pressure will start to build up. Continue heating until the required pressure has been reached, as indicated by one of the three rings on the plunger inside the weight. When pressure has been reached, reduce the heat to maintain the indicator ring in the correct position. Start calculating the cooking time from here.*
3. *After cooking, as the cooker cools, the pressure subsides and the indicator rings disappear into the weight. When the rings have subsided into the weight rattle the weight slightly with the aid of a fork to make sure all hissing has stopped, remove the weight then remove the lid.*

3

Type 2 (eg Tower) As pressure subsides the indicator rings disappear into the weight. When the rings have subsided into the weight rattle the weight slightly with a fork to make sure all hissing has stopped then remove the weight and lid.

Type 3 (eg Tefal) Remove the cooker from the heat and lift the rotating valve slightly to the first notch. This allows the steam to escape gently from the cooker until pressure has been reduced. There is no slow or quick method.

Pressure has subsided when all steam has escaped. Don't let the cooker cool without first releasing the pressure. If you do a vacuum will be created by the condensing steam and you will be unable to lift the lid. If this happens accidentally, reheat the cooker again before attempting to remove the lid.

Cooking more than one food at a time
When cooking several foods together, make use of the trivet and separators. When cooking braised meat with accompanying vegetables, for example, gently place the trivet on top of the meat, then place the vegetables in separators and put them on top of the trivet.

It is useful to have an extra trivet to act as a separator between different foods, and to stand vegetable separators on. If, for example, you are cooking a bacon joint on the trivet in the bottom of the cooker, you could place the spare trivet on top and stand on it vegetables or rice in a separator, or fish wrapped in foil.

It is important to make sure that the cooker is not over filled, as there must be room for the steam to circulate.

Care and cleaning

Here are some general points. For more detail consult the manufacturer's handbook.

1. After use, wash the whole cooker in hot, sudsy water as for ordinary saucepans. Rinse in warm water and dry thoroughly. Check that the air vent and pipe are clear. If they become blocked, clear them under a strong jet of water.

2. Do not use an abrasive cleaner, steel wool or soap filled pads, on a coloured surface as it will cause scratching.

3. Non-stick models should be treated in the same way as other non-stick pans. Wash in hot sudsy water and use a sponge or plastic scourer to remove awkward spots. Do not use scouring powder. Avoid using metal utensils when cooking, and use only medium heat when frying food.

4. Hard water may discolour the interior of the base (unless it is non-stick). This can be avoided by adding a little vinegar or lemon juice to the water when cooking any food which is to be steamed,

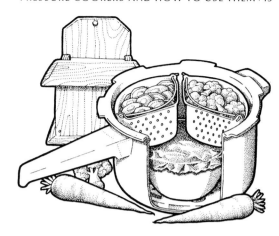

Packing a main course and vegetables in a Hi-dome cooker

but do not do this when the liquid is to be used for sauce or gravy. If the cooker does become discoloured, the stain can be removed separately with soap filled pads or by boiling a few pieces of rhubarb or apple peelings in the cooker.

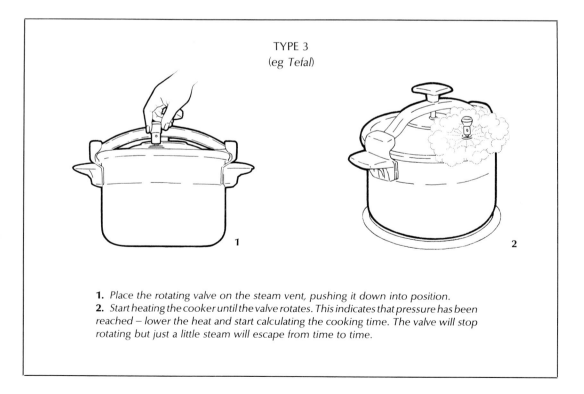

TYPE 3
(eg *Tefal*)

1

2

1. *Place the rotating valve on the steam vent, pushing it down into position.*
2. *Start heating the cooker until the valve rotates. This indicates that pressure has been reached – lower the heat and start calculating the cooking time. The valve will stop rotating but just a little steam will escape from time to time.*

*Pressure cooker (Hi-dome model)
showing separators and
food in position*

from some hardware stores or direct from the manufacturer.

Dos, don'ts and hints

The liquid used for pressure cooking must be one which produces steam when it boils, with the exception of Type 3 (eg Tefal). See manufacturer's instructions.

Never use less than the recommended quantity of liquid. The quantity of liquid depends on the length of cooking time, not on the amount of food being cooked. The total amount of liquid required for the recipe should be put in the cooker before it is brought to pressure.

Carry out any preliminary frying in the cooker without the lid.

Thickening is best carried out after cooking rather than before.

Do not overfill the pressure cooker. Most models should not be more than two thirds filled with solid food and only half filled with liquids.

Make sure the lid is correctly closed.

Time the cooking accurately – use a 'pinger' timer.

Do not try to remove the weight or lid before pressure has been reduced.

Do not put foods requiring different cooking times in the cooker at the same time. If, for example, accompanying vegetables take less time than the meat, reduce the pressure part of the way through the cooking time, add the vegetables, bring to pressure again and continue cooking for the required time.

Read the recipe carefully: follow instructions.

Follow recipe instructions for reducing pressure (on page 13 we explain why this is important).

When buying meat on the bone check that you are not paying top price for the bone.

Cut meat and vegetables into pieces as even-sized as possible for best results.

Careful browning of meat and veg is vital to ensure a good colour and flavour to the dish.

All frying should be done in the *open* pressure cooker.

Where the recipe calls for chicken joints, it is often cheaper to buy a whole chicken and joint it rather than buy ready jointed pieces.

Add seasoning *after* the main ingredients and stock have been added – not before.

5. Store the cooker with the lid inverted to allow air to circulate and prevent a musty smell. Make sure the cooker does not get knocked against other pans, as this may damage the rim and prevent it sealing.

6. When cooking, avoid tapping the rim of the cooker with metal spoons or handles, as this may damage it.

7. Remove and wash the rubber sealing gasket frequently and dry it thoroughly before putting it back. Examine it now and again to make sure the 'rubber' shows no sign of perishing. If it does become damaged, or if you notice steam escaping from the rim during cooking, replace the gasket with a new one.

8. Check replacement parts periodically and replace when necessary. It is useful to keep a spare set of parts in the kitchen. They can be obtained

SOUPS AND STOCKS

Although canned and packet soups are useful convenience foods, they are an expensive way of providing for the family. Far more nutritious, flavoursome and economical family soups can be made in a pressure cooker with little more time than it takes to reheat one from a packet. A blender is useful to purée the vegetables, but sieving will achieve the same result, although it takes a little longer.

The basis of all good soups and stews is a good stock. Stock cubes can be used (if you use stock cubes, remember to cut down on additional seasoning) but most households have leftover meat bones from joints or poultry carcasses. With the addition of a few fresh vegetables and herbs, an excellent stock can be made in a pressure cooker in far less time than usual. The basic household stock is suitable for most dishes, but recipes are also included here for other stocks required for specific recipes.

Rules for making stock in a pressure cooker
1. Do not use the trivet.
2. Bring the stock to the boil and skim before finally bringing to pressure.
3. Do not have the cooker more than half full when all ingredients and liquid have been added.
4. Do not include cooked vegetables and starchy

Making stock in a Hi-dome cooker

foods, because they disintegrate and make the stock cloudy.
5. Tie the herbs (bouquet garni) in a piece of muslin, for easy removal when the stock is made.
6. The resulting stock is very concentrated (well jellied), which makes it easier for storing. When required, dilute it with an equal quantity of water or vegetable liquid.
7. Keep stock in the refrigerator and reboil it every other day to keep it in good condition or when cold store in a freezer.

Basic household stock

900 g (2 lb) bones from fresh or cooked meat
1·4 litres (2 ½ pints) water
2 onions, skinned and sliced
2 carrots, scraped and sliced
2 sticks of celery, washed and sliced
5 ml (1 level tsp) salt
4 peppercorns
bouquet garni

Wash the bones and chop them into small pieces. Put the bones in the pressure cooker with the water. Bring to the boil uncovered and remove the scum. Add the prepared vegetables, salt, peppercorns and bouquet garni. Put on the lid, bring to high (15 lb) pressure, then cook for 1–1 ¼ hours. Reduce pressure slowly. Strain the stock through a colander into a clean container. Allow to cool, and skim off the fat when cold.

If marrow bones are used, increase the water to 1·7 litres (3 pints) and cook for 2 hours.

Bouquet garni

1 bayleaf
1 sprig of fresh parsley, or 2·5 ml (½ level tsp) dried parsley
1 sprig of fresh thyme, or 2·5 ml (½ level tsp) dried thyme
1 sprig of fresh marjoram, or 2·5 ml (½ level tsp) dried marjoram

Wrap the herbs in a small piece of muslin and tie with a piece of fine string.

Brown stock

450 g (1 lb) marrow bone or knuckle of veal,
  chopped
450 g (1 lb) shin of beef, cut into pieces
1·4 litres (2½ pints) water
1 carrot, scraped and sliced
1 onion, skinned and sliced
1 stick of celery, washed and sliced
2·5 ml (½ level tsp) salt
4 peppercorns

To give extra flavour and colour, brown the bones
and meat in the oven. Put the bones and meat in
the cooker with the water, vegetables, salt and
peppercorns, bring to the boil uncovered and
remove the scum. Put on the lid, bring to high (15
lb) pressure, then cook for 1–1¼ hours. Reduce
pressure slowly. Strain the stock and leave it to
cool. When cold, remove the fat from the stock.

White stock

900 g (2 lb) knuckle of veal, chopped
1·4 litres (2½ pints) cold water
15 ml (1 tbsp) lemon juice
1 onion, skinned and sliced
1 carrot, scraped and sliced
bouquet garni
5 ml (1 level tsp) salt

Put knuckle in the pressure cooker with the water
and lemon juice. Bring to the boil uncovered and
remove scum. Add the rest of the ingredients. Put
on the lid and bring to high (15 lb) pressure, then
cook for 1–1½ hours. Reduce pressure slowly.
Strain the stock and leave it to cool. When the
stock is cold remove the fat.

Vegetable stock

100 g (4 oz) onions, skinned and sliced
100 g (4 oz) carrots, scraped and sliced
2 sticks of celery, washed and sliced
50 g (2 oz) swede or turnip, peeled and sliced
1 leek, sliced and washed
bouquet garni
5 ml (1 level tsp) salt
4 peppercorns
1·4 litres (2½ pints) cold water

Put all ingredients in the pressure cooker and bring
to the boil uncovered. Remove any scum. Put on

lid, bring to high (15 lb) pressure, then cook for 15
minutes. Reduce pressure slowly. Strain the stock.

Chicken stock

1 chicken carcass, fresh or cooked
chicken giblets
1 onion, skinned and sliced
1 stick of celery, washed and sliced
1 carrot, scraped and sliced
1·1 litres (2 pints) water
5 ml (1 level tsp) salt
bouquet garni
4 peppercorns

Break up the carcass. Put carcass, with any skin or
trimmings, in the pressure cooker and add the
washed giblets and all other ingredients. Bring to
the boil uncovered and remove the scum. Put on
the lid and bring to high (15 lb) pressure, then cook
for 45 minutes if using a cooked carcass, 60
minutes if using a fresh carcass. Reduce pressure
slowly, strain the stock and leave to cool. When
cold, remove the fat.

Fish stock

1 cod's head or fish bones and trimmings
900 ml (1½ pints) water
1 onion, skinned and sliced
1 stick of celery, washed and sliced
5 ml (1 level tsp) salt
bouquet garni
4 peppercorns
2 blades of mace

Wash the fish and put in the pressure cooker with
all the other ingredients. Bring to the boil uncovered and remove the scum. Put on the lid and
bring to high (15 lb) pressure, then cook for 10
minutes. Reduce pressure slowly. Strain the stock.

Leek and potato soup

225 g (8 oz) potatoes, peeled and sliced
225 g (8 oz) leeks, sliced and washed
100 g (4 oz) onion, skinned and sliced
25 g (1 oz) butter or margarine
900 ml (1½ pints) stock
2·5 ml (½ level tsp) grated nutmeg
1 bayleaf
salt and pepper
30 ml (2 tbsp) cream or top of milk

Fry the vegetables in the fat for 1 minute in the uncovered pressure cooker. Add the stock, nutmeg, bayleaf and seasoning. Put on the lid and bring to high (15 lb) pressure. Cook for 5 minutes. Reduce pressure quickly. Remove the bayleaf and sieve the soup, or purée it in an electric blender. Return the soup to the pan, add the cream and reheat. Serve with toast or croûtons.

SERVES 8

Lentil soup

25 g (1 oz) butter or margarine
100 g (4 oz) lentils, washed
2 medium-size onions, skinned and chopped
2 sticks of celery, washed, trimmed and chopped
2 medium-size potatoes, peeled and diced
700 ml (1 ¼ pints) water
1 bacon knuckle, bacon pieces or bones
bouquet garni
salt and pepper
about 150 ml (¼ pint) milk
15 ml (1 tbsp) chopped parsley and fried croûtons
for garnish

Melt the butter to grease the bottom of the pressure cooker. Add the lentils and vegetables and stir well. Pour on the water and bring to the boil uncovered, and stir again to ensure the lentils have not stuck to the base. Put in the bacon, bouquet garni and seasoning. Put on the lid and bring to high (15 lb) pressure. Cook for 15 minutes. Reduce the pressure slowly. Remove any bacon bones or skin and the bouquet garni. Sieve the soup or purée it in an electric blender, then return it to the pan with the milk and reheat. Adjust the seasoning and serve with parsley and croûtons.

SERVES 8

Bortsch

Bortsch may also be served chilled with a whirl of soured cream on the top.

4 raw beetroots about 450 g (1 lb) peeled and
coarsely grated
2 medium-size onions, skinned and finely chopped
1·1 litres (2 pints) brown stock
salt and pepper
30 ml (2 tbsp) lemon juice
90 ml (6 tbsp) dry sherry
142-ml (¼-pint) carton of soured cream

Put the beetroots in the pressure cooker with the onions, stock, salt and pepper. Put on the lid and bring to high (15 lb) pressure. Cook for 15 minutes. Reduce pressure quickly. Sieve the soup or purée it in an electric blender. Return it to the pan and reheat. Adjust seasoning and stir in the lemon juice and sherry. Just before serving, stir in half the soured cream. Serve the soup in hot dishes with the remaining cream spooned on to the individual servings.

SERVES 8

Fresh tomato soup

900 g (2 lb) tomatoes, skinned and chopped
1 clove of garlic, skinned and crushed
225 g (8 oz) onions, skinned and chopped
1 stick of celery, washed, trimmed and sliced
25 g (1 oz) butter or margarine
600 ml (1 pint) vegetable stock or water
bouquet garni
salt and pepper
30 ml (2 level tbsp) tomato paste
10 ml (2 level tsp) sugar
chopped chives or watercress
30 ml (2 tbsp) sherry, optional

Fry the tomatoes, garlic, onions and celery in the fat in the uncovered cooker for 2 minutes. Add the stock, bouquet garni, salt, pepper, tomato paste and sugar. Put on the lid and bring to high (15 lb) pressure, then cook for 6 minutes. Reduce pressure quickly. Remove bouquet garni. Sieve the soup or purée it in an electric blender and return it to the pan to reheat. Adjust the seasoning and serve sprinkled with chopped chives or watercress. If wished, add sherry before serving.

SERVES 8

Creamy artichoke soup

900 g (2 lb) Jerusalem artichokes
4 medium-size onions, skinned and chopped
bayleaf
salt and pepper
600 ml (1 pint) white stock or chicken stock
25 g (1 oz) butter or margarine
25 g (1 oz) flour
300 ml (½ pint) milk
30 ml (2 tbsp) cream
30 ml (2 tbsp) dry sherry

Wash and peel the artichokes and keep them in cold water until required. Slice the artichokes and put them in the pressure cooker with the onions, bayleaf, salt, pepper and stock. Put on the lid and bring to high (15 lb) pressure, then cook for 5 minutes. Reduce pressure quickly. Remove the bayleaf. Sieve the vegetables or purée in an electric blender.

Melt the fat in the rinsed out cooker, stir in the flour and cook uncovered for 2–3 minutes. Remove cooker from the heat and gradually stir in the milk. Bring to the boil uncovered and continue stirring until the liquid thickens. Add the artichoke purée, reheat to boiling point and adjust the seasoning. Just before serving, stir in the cream and sherry. Serve with croûtons or anchovy twists.
SERVES 8

Hotch potch

A good healthy winter soup – as the main course of the meal it will give about eight generous helpings.

225 g (8 oz) Jerusalem artichokes
1 bacon rasher, rinded and chopped
25 g (1 oz) butter or margarine
50 g (2 oz) split peas
225 g (8 oz) carrots, scraped and sliced
100 g (4 oz) swede or turnip, peeled and sliced
4 medium-size onions, skinned and chopped
2 stalks of celery, washed and sliced
1·7 litres (3 pints) brown stock or water
15 ml (1 level tbsp) tomato paste
bouquet garni
salt and pepper
30 ml (2 tbsp) chopped parsley

Peel the artichokes and keep in cold water until required. Lightly fry the bacon in the fat in the uncovered pressure cooker, then stir in the split peas until well coated with fat. Add the rest of the vegetables, the stock, tomato paste, bouquet garni and seasoning. Bring to boiling point uncovered and stir well. Put on the lid and bring to high (15 lb) pressure. Cook for 15 minutes. Reduce pressure slowly. Remove the bouquet garni. Sieve the soup or purée it in an electric blender, then return it to the pan and reheat. Adjust seasoning and serve sprinkled with chopped parsley.
SERVES ABOUT 8

Split pea and bacon soup

Soak the bacon knuckle in cold water for at least 2 hours before using it.

25 g (1 oz) butter or margarine
100 g (4 oz) split peas
1 clove of garlic, skinned and crushed
2 medium-size onions, skinned and chopped
225 g (8 oz) tomatoes, skinned and chopped, or
    45 ml (3 level tbsp) tomato paste
1 bacon knuckle about 450 g (1 lb), soaked
salt and pepper
1·1 litres (2 pints) water
60 ml (4 level tbsp) fried breadcrumbs
60 ml (4 level tbsp) coarsely grated cheese

Melt the fat so that it greases the bottom of the pressure cooker. Stir in the split peas, garlic and vegetables so that they are coated with fat. Add the bacon, salt, pepper and water. Bring to the boil uncovered and stir well. Put on the lid and bring to high (15 lb) pressure. Cook for 15 minutes. Reduce pressure slowly. Remove the bacon knuckle and skin it. Cut the meat from the bone and dice it. Sieve the soup or purée it in an electric blender, then return it to the pan with the bacon. Reheat and adjust seasoning. Serve sprinkled with the fried crumbs and cheese.
SERVES 8

Cream of celery soup

1 large head of celery, washed, trimmed and sliced
1 medium-size onion, skinned and sliced
25 g (1 oz) butter or margarine
700 ml (1 ¼ pints) white or vegetable stock
salt and pepper
bouquet garni
45 ml (3 level tbsp) flour
150 ml (¼ pint) milk
45 ml (3 tbsp) cream
chopped parsley

Fry the vegetables lightly in the fat in the uncovered pressure cooker for about 2 minutes. Add the stock, seasoning and bouquet garni. Put on the lid, bring to high (15 lb) pressure, then cook for 5 minutes. Reduce pressure quickly. Remove the bouquet garni. Sieve the soup or purée it in an electric blender. Return it to the cooker and bring to the boil uncovered. Blend the flour and milk to a

smooth cream and stir in a little of the hot soup: add this mixture to the cooker and reboil uncovered, stirring until the soup thickens. Cook uncovered for 2 minutes, adjust the seasoning and add the cream and chopped parsley. Serve with croûtons or toast.
SERVES 6–8

Cream of onion soup

Fried crisp onion rings make an attractive garnish for this soup.

700 g (1 ½ lb) onions, skinned and sliced
25 g (1 oz) butter or margarine
600 ml (1 pint) white stock
bouquet garni
salt and pepper
45 ml (3 level tbsp) flour
300 ml (½ pint) milk
60–75 ml (4–5 tbsp) cream

Lightly fry the onions in the fat in the uncovered cooker for about 2 minutes. Add the stock, bouquet garni, salt and pepper. Put on the lid and bring to high (15 lb) pressure, then cook for 4 minutes. Reduce the pressure quickly. Remove the bouquet garni. Sieve the onions or purée them in an electric blender. Return them to the pan and reheat. Blend the flour and milk to a smooth cream, stir in a little hot soup, then add mixture to the pan and bring to the boil uncovered. Adjust the seasoning. Stir in the cream just before serving.
SERVES 6–8

Green pea soup

This soup can be made with 350 g (12 oz) frozen peas instead of the fresh ones.

900 g (2 lb) fresh peas in pods
2 medium-size onions, skinned and chopped
1 sprig of mint
50 g (2 oz) spinach, if available
900 ml (1 ½ pints) white stock or chicken stock
salt and pepper
45 ml (3 level tbsp) flour
150 ml (¼ pint) milk
10 ml (2 level tsp) sugar
90 ml (6 tbsp) double cream

Wash the peas and shell about 20 pods. Tie the shelled peas in muslin to use for the garnish later. Put the rest of the pods, onions, mint, spinach, stock, salt, pepper and garnish in the cooker. Put on the lid and bring to high (15 lb) pressure, then cook for 5 minutes. Reduce pressure quickly. Remove the garnish and sprig of mint. Sieve the soup or purée it in an electric blender (if the purée is fibrous, it is better to pass it through a sieve as well). Return the mixture to the pan and reheat. Blend the flour and milk to a smooth cream. Stir in a little of the hot liquid and add it to the rest of the soup. Bring to the boil, stirring until the soup thickens and cook for 2–3 minutes. Add the sugar and adjust the seasoning. Stir in the garnish of peas and the lightly whipped cream just before serving.
SERVES 6–8

Cream of chicken soup

A few mixed vegetables such as cooked peas, diced carrots and swede or turnip may be used as an extra garnish for this soup.

1 chicken carcass from roast chicken
chicken giblets
1 stick of celery, washed, trimmed and sliced
2 medium-size onions, skinned and chopped
50 g (2 oz) mushroom stalks, washed and chopped
bouquet garni
1·1 litres (2 pints) water
50 g (2 oz) butter or margarine
50 g (2 oz) flour
300 ml (½ pint) milk
grated nutmeg
30 ml (2 tbsp) cream

Remove all scraps of meat from the carcass, cut them into neat pieces and set aside. Crush the carcass and put it in the pressure cooker with the giblets, vegetables, bouquet garni and the water. Put on the lid and bring to high (15 lb) pressure, then cook for 45 minutes. Reduce pressure quickly. Strain the stock, leave it to cool, then discard the chicken fat.

Melt the fat in a pan, stir in the flour, and cook for 2–3 minutes. Remove pan from the heat and stir in the milk and 900 ml (1 ½ pints) chicken stock. Return pan to the heat and bring to the boil, stirring until the soup thickens. Add the meat trimmings and nutmeg. Just before serving, stir in the cream. Serve with croûtons or toast.

SERVES 6–8

Hearty bean soup

This filling soup will make a main meal, serving about eight people.

175 g (6 oz) haricot beans
1·7 litres (3 pints) water
1 large carrot, scraped and sliced
2 medium-size onions, skinned and chopped
2 sticks of celery, washed, trimmed and sliced
100 g (4 oz) cabbage, washed and shredded
454-g (1-lb) can of tomatoes
bouquet garni
salt and pepper
2·5 ml (1 level tsp) dry mustard
15 ml (1 tbsp) vinegar
1 hardboiled egg, chopped
1 lemon, sliced

Pour 600 ml (1 pint) boiling water over the beans and leave to soak for two hours. Drain the beans and put them in the pressure cooker with all other

Preparing minestrone soup

ingredients except the egg and lemon. Put on the lid and bring to high (15 lb) pressure. Cook for 15 minutes. Reduce the pressure slowly. Remove the bouquet garni. Sieve the soup or purée it in an electric blender. Return the soup to the pan, adjust the seasoning and bring to boiling point. Serve garnished with the chopped hardboiled egg and slices of lemon.

Minestrone soup

Other vegetables such as peas, green beans, haricot or red beans may be used in the soup as variations. If dried vegetables are used, they should be soaked and half cooked before being added to the soup.

1 small leek, shredded and washed
1 onion, skinned and finely chopped
2 bacon rashers, rinded and chopped
1 clove of garlic, skinned and crushed
25 g (1 oz) butter or margarine
700 ml (1 ¼ pints) white stock
1 large carrot, scraped and diced
1 small turnip or swede, peeled and diced
1 stick of celery, washed, trimmed and diced
45 ml (3 tbsp) shortcut macaroni
100 g (4 oz) cabbage, washed and finely shredded
15 ml (1 level tbsp) tomato paste
bayleaf
salt and pepper
grated Parmesan cheese

Lightly fry the leek, onion, bacon and garlic in the fat in the uncovered pressure cooker. Add the other ingredients, except the cheese, put on the lid and bring to high (15 lb) pressure. Cook for 7 minutes. Reduce pressure slowly. Remove the bayleaf. Serve the soup with plenty of grated cheese.

SERVES 8

Cock-a-leekie

1 chicken, about 1 kg (2 ¼ lb)
700 ml (1 ¼ pints) water
225 g (8 oz) leeks, sliced and washed
salt and pepper
100 g (4 oz) long grain rice

Put the wiped chicken in the pressure cooker with

the water, leeks and seasoning. Put on the lid and bring to high (15 lb) pressure. Cook for 20 minutes. Reduce pressure quickly. Cut the meat off the bones in large chunks and return it to the cooker. Add the rice, bring to high (15 lb) pressure, then cook for 5 minutes. Reduce pressure slowly. Serve the soup with thick slices of crusty bread.
SERVES 6

Oxtail soup with dumplings

As oxtail tends to be fatty, partly cook the soup and allow it to stand for 12 hours to allow the fat to settle and set, so that it can be removed. Finish cooking the soup just before it is required. The soup is a meal in itself.

1 oxtail, jointed
25 g (1 oz) butter or margarine
2 onions, skinned and chopped
1 carrot, scraped and sliced
25 g (1 oz) lean ham or bacon
1·1 litres (2 pints) brown stock
bouquet garni
salt and pepper
chopped parsley to garnish

For the dumplings
100 g (4 oz) self raising flour
2·5 ml (½ level tsp) salt
50 g (2 oz) chopped suet
about 75 ml (5 tbsp) cold water

Wipe the oxtail and trim off excess fat. Fry the pieces in butter or margarine in the uncovered pressure cooker, with the vegetables and bacon, for about 5 minutes. Remove cooker from heat, pour on the stock and add the bouquet garni and seasoning. (Take care not to over fill the cooker at this stage.) Put on the lid and bring to high (15 lb) pressure, then cook for 40 minutes. Reduce pressure quickly. Strain the soup, remove the meat from bones, discard bones and add meat to the soup with the vegetables, excluding the bouquet garni. Leave soup to cool and allow the fat to set.

Make the dumplings by mixing the dry ingredients to a soft dough with the cold water. Shape the dough into balls. Remove fat from the soup. Return the soup to the pressure cooker and bring it to the boil uncovered. Adjust the seasoning. Drop in the dumplings, put the lid on the cooker without the weight and gently reboil until a steady flow of steam is passing through the vent. Lower the heat and allow the dumplings to steam gently for 2 minutes. Then increase the heat to bring to low (5 lb) pressure. Cook for 5 minutes. Reduce pressure slowly. Serve the soup sprinkled with coarsely chopped parsley.
SERVES 4–6

Goulash soup

350 g (¾ lb) stewing steak or leg of beef
5 ml (1 level tsp) salt
freshly ground black pepper
25 g (1 oz) butter or margarine
1 large onion, skinned and chopped
226-g (8-oz) can of tomatoes
63-g (2¼-oz) can of tomato paste
600 ml (1 pint) beef stock
15 ml (1 level tbsp) paprika pepper
450 g (1 lb) potatoes, peeled
142-ml (¼-pint) carton of soured cream

Trim the meat, cut it into small pieces and season well. Melt the fat in the uncovered pressure cooker, add onion and cook until soft; about 5 minutes. Add meat, tomatoes, tomato paste, beef stock and paprika to the pressure cooker. Stir to blend ingredients together. Put lid on pressure cooker, bring to high (15 lb) pressure, then cook for 15 minutes. Reduce pressure quickly. Cut potatoes into bite size pieces and add them to the soup. Put the lid on the pressure cooker, bring back to high (15 lb) pressure, then cook for 4–5 minutes. Reduce pressure quickly. Serve soup and pour soured cream into each portion.
SERVES 6

French onion soup

350 g (12 oz) onions, skinned and sliced
50 g (2 oz) butter or margarine
700 ml (1¼ pints) chicken stock
bayleaf
salt and pepper
4 slices of French bread
grated Gruyère or Cheddar cheese
30 ml (2 tbsp) dry sherry

French onion soup

Lightly fry the onions in the fat in the uncovered pressure cooker until soft and lightly browned. Add the stock, bayleaf and seasoning. Put on the lid and bring to high (15 lb) pressure, then cook for 5 minutes. Reduce pressure quickly. Remove the bayleaf.

Toast the bread, sprinkle it thickly with cheese and brown it under the grill. Reheat the soup, adjust the seasoning, stir in the sherry and serve in individual dishes with the toast floating on top.

Fish and corn chowder

2 rashers of bacon, rinded and chopped
25 g (1 oz) butter or margarine
1 onion, skinned and sliced
1 stalk of celery, washed, trimmed and chopped
2 potatoes, about 100 g (4 oz) peeled and diced
600 ml (1 pint) fish stock
bayleaf
350 g (12 oz) conger eel, skinned and cubed
100 g (4 oz) fresh or frozen sweetcorn
salt and pepper
30 ml (2 level tbsp) flour
300 ml (½ pint) milk
chopped parsley

Lightly fry the bacon in the fat in the uncovered

pressure cooker. Add the onion, celery and potatoes and sauté for a further minute. Add the fish stock, bayleaf, eel, corn, salt and pepper. Put on the lid and bring to high (15 lb) pressure, then cook for 8 minutes. Reduce pressure slowly. Remove the bayleaf and adjust seasoning. Blend the flour to a cream with a little cold milk, stir in some of the hot fish liquid, then add mixture to the pan with the remaining milk and bring to the boil. Serve sprinkled with chopped parsley.

Curried cod chowder

50 g (2 oz) butter or margarine
1 large onion, skinned and chopped
2 sticks of celery, washed, trimmed and chopped
2·5 ml (½ level tsp) curry powder
45 ml (3 level tbsp) flour
300 ml (½ pint) milk
900 ml (1½ pints) water
2 large potatoes, peeled and diced
700 g (1½ lb) cod fillet or any white fish, skinned
salt and pepper
chopped parsley and chives

Melt the fat in the pressure cooker, add the onion and celery and cook uncovered until the onion is soft, about 3 minutes. Stir in the curry powder and flour and cook for 1 minute, stirring. Remove the cooker from the heat and gradually stir in the milk and water. Add the potatoes, fish and seasoning. Stir to mix the ingredients. Put the lid on the cooker, bring up to high (15 lb) pressure, then cook for 4–5 minutes. Reduce pressure quickly. Stir in the parsley and chives and serve immediately.
SERVES 8

Cream of fish soup

350 g (12 oz) whiting, coley, cod or haddock
600 ml (1 pint) fish stock
bayleaf
salt and pepper
25 g (1 oz) butter or margarine
25 g (1 oz) flour
300 ml (½ pint) milk
25 g (1 oz) peeled prawns, roughly chopped
90 ml (6 tbsp) double cream
paprika pepper

Wash and wipe the fish and cut it into pieces. Put

the fish in the pressure cooker with the stock, bayleaf and seasoning. Put on the lid and bring to high (15 lb) pressure. Cook for 2 minutes. Reduce the pressure quickly. Strain the stock into a jug. Remove all skin and bones from the fish and discard. Remove the bayleaf. Sieve the fish or purée it in an electric blender with some of the stock.

Melt the fat in the cooker, stir in the flour and cook uncovered for about 2 minutes. Remove cooker from the heat and stir in the remaining stock and milk. Return cooker to the heat and bring the liquid to the boil, stirring until it thickens. Stir in the fish purée and adjust the seasoning. Just before serving, stir in the prawns and lightly whipped cream. Sprinkle with paprika pepper.

Scotch broth

700 g (1 ½ lb) shin of beef
1·7 litres (3 pints) water
1 large carrot, scraped and finely diced
½ small turnip, peeled and finely diced
½ small swede, peeled and finely diced
1 large onion, skinned and chopped
2 leeks, thinly sliced and washed
45 ml (3 level tbsp) pearl barley
salt and pepper
30 ml (2 tbsp) chopped parsley

Cut the meat into 2·5-cm (1-in) pieces and put it in the pressure cooker with the water, bring to the boil uncovered and remove any scum. Then add the prepared vegetables, barley and seasoning. Stir well to ensure that the barley is not sticking to the base. Put on the lid and bring to high (15 lb) pressure. Cook for 25 minutes. Reduce pressure slowly. Adjust seasoning. Serve sprinkled with chopped parsley.

SERVES 8

Chicken broth

1 small carrot, scraped and diced
1 medium-size onion, skinned and diced
1 stalk of celery, washed, trimmed and diced
1 small leek, finely shredded and washed
1·1 litres (2 pints) chicken stock
bayleaf
salt and pepper
25 g (1 oz) long grain rice
chopped parsley

Put all the vegetables and stock in the pressure cooker. Add the bayleaf and seasoning, bring to the boil uncovered, and skim if necessary. Stir in the rice and bring to the boil again, stirring. Put on the lid and bring to high (15 lb) pressure, then cook for 6 minutes. Reduce pressure slowly. Adjust seasoning and remove bayleaf. Serve sprinkled with chopped parsley.

SERVES 8

FISH RECIPES

Fish cooked in a pressure cooker is either poached or steamed. It may seem unnecessary to do this in a pressure cooker, as fish does not normally require long cooking by those methods, but pressure cooking has several advantages. Not only does it cut down on time but it reduces the smell of fish in the kitchen and retains the full flavour of the fish. The concentrated stock from the cooking can be used for an accompanying sauce or for fish soup.

As pressure cooked fish is ready in such a short time, it is ideal for a quickly prepared meal. Choose a vegetable which needs the same cooking time as the fish or one which can be cooked while the finishing sauces or garnishes are made. Small new potatoes, for example, can be cooked in the same time as many types of fish. For creamed potatoes, cut old potatoes in slices and cook them in the pressure cooker with the fish, then cream them after.

Cooking methods

There are three basic methods for cooking fish under pressure. It is advisable to use the trivet for all methods and 150–300 ml (¼–½ pint) of water, or other liquid specified in the recipe, according to the type and size of the cooker. (Remember to follow the manufacturer's instructions when deciding the minimum quantity of liquid required.) Clean, trim and wash the fish before cooking. Use one of the following methods.

1. Place the fish on the trivet and cook for the required time. The remaining fish stock can be used to make an accompanying sauce.
2. Put the fish in an ovenproof or flameproof serving dish or casserole, that will fit easily into the cooker, with accompanying vegetables and flavourings, and cook according to the recipe.
3. Parcel the fish in foil with seasonings and a little liquid and cook for the required time. Both large pieces of fish and individual portions can be cooked in this way.

In the last two methods the fish cooks mainly in its own juices and therefore retains its full flavour and nutrients.

Cooking frozen fish

Frozen fish is already prepared for cooking and it does not have to be thawed before pressure cooking. It can be cooked for the same time as stated in the recipes or timetable.

Turbot bonne femme

Other white fish, such as plaice fillets, sole, halibut and hake, may be used in place of turbot. Adjust the cooking time accordingly (see chart page 32).

40 g (1 ½ oz) butter
4 pieces of turbot about 175 g (6 oz) each
2 shallots, skinned and chopped
100 g (4 oz) button mushrooms
45 ml (3 tbsp) dry white wine
salt and pepper
bayleaf
30 ml (2 level tbsp) flour
about 150 ml (¼ pint) milk
60 ml (4 tbsp) cream

Grease a large piece of foil with a very little of the butter and place the washed and trimmed steaks of turbot on it (black skin uppermost). Sprinkle with the shallots and finely chopped stalks from the mushrooms. Spoon the wine over the fish, sprinkle with salt and pepper and put in the bayleaf. Fold the foil into a neat parcel, sealing the ends well so that the fish juices cannot escape. Put the trivet in the pressure cooker and put in 300 ml (½ pint) water. Place the foil parcel on the trivet. Put on the lid and bring to high (15 lb) pressure. Cook for 5–6 minutes. Reduce pressure quickly. Remove the parcel of fish, carefully undo it; strain off the cooking liquid and reserve. Remove the black skin from the turbot, arrange it in a hot dish and keep it warm.

Meanwhile make the sauce. Lightly fry sliced mushrooms in half the butter in a pan. When cooked, put the mushrooms with the fish, keeping a few for garnish. Add the remaining butter to the pan and stir in the flour. Cook for 2–3 minutes. Remove the pan from the heat and gradually stir in the cooking liquid made up to 300 ml (½ pint) with the milk. Bring to the boil, stirring until the sauce thickens. Cook gently for about 2 minutes. Remove the pan from the heat and stir in the cream. Pour the sauce over the fish and garnish with extra mushrooms.

Salmon hollandaise

4 salmon cutlets about 175 g (6 oz) each
salt and pepper
60 ml (4 tbsp) dry white wine
450 g (1 lb) new potatoes, scraped
2–3 sprigs of mint
5 ml (1 level tsp) sugar
350 g (12 oz) peas, shelled

For the hollandaise sauce

30 ml (2 tbsp) vinegar
30 ml (2 tbsp) lemon juice
6 peppercorns
bayleaf
blade of mace
2 egg yolks
100 g (4 oz) butter, softened

First start to prepare the hollandaise sauce. Put the vinegar, lemon juice, peppercorns, bayleaf and blade of mace in a small pan and simmer for about 5 minutes until reduced to about 15 ml (1 tbsp). Strain the mixture into a basin which is standing over a pan of hot (not boiling) water. Have ready the egg yolks and butter.

Butter four pieces of foil and put a salmon cutlet on each. Sprinkle with salt and pepper and put about 15 ml (1 tbsp) wine over each. Wrap into neat parcels. Put the trivet in the pressure cooker and pour in 300 ml (½ pint) water. Stand the parcels of fish on the trivet.

Put the potatoes in a vegetable separator, sprinkle with salt and put a few sprigs of mint with them. Stand the separator on the fish parcels in the cooker. Put on the lid and bring to high (15 lb) pressure. Cook for 3 minutes. Reduce pressure quickly.

Put the peas in a vegetable separator, sprinkle with salt, sugar and add a sprig of mint. Place

Salmon hollandaise

separator in the cooker. Put on the lid and bring to high (15 lb) pressure. Cook for a further 3 minutes.

Meanwhile finish the hollandaise sauce. Put the pan of hot water containing the basin of spiced vinegar over the heat, and bring the water to just below boiling point. While it is heating, whisk the egg yolks into the vinegar. As the mixture thickens, gradually whisk in the butter in small pieces. The sauce should be thick and fluffy. Adjust the seasoning.

Reduce the pressure in the cooker quickly. Remove the fish and undo the foil. Serve the salmon on a hot plate with the juices poured over and the peas and potatoes arranged round it. Serve the hollandaise sauce separately.

Whiting casserole

1 medium-size onion, skinned and finely chopped
25 g (1 oz) almonds, blanched and split
1 stalk of celery, washed, trimmed and finely chopped
1 carrot, scraped and coarsely grated
50 g (2 oz) butter or margarine
175 g (6 oz) long grain rice
100 g (4 oz) mushrooms, sliced
salt and pepper
30 ml (2 level tbsp) tomato paste
450 ml (¾ pint) fish stock or chicken stock
4 whiting, filleted, skinned and cubed
15 ml (1 tbsp) chopped parsley

Lightly fry the onion, almonds, celery and carrot

in half the fat in a pan. When just brown, stir in the remaining butter, add the rice and mushrooms and continue cooking until the rice has absorbed the fat. Sprinkle with seasoning and put into a casserole that will fit easily into the pressure cooker. Mix together the tomato paste and stock and pour it into the casserole. Cover with a piece of foil.

Put the trivet in the pressure cooker and pour in 300 ml (½ pint) water. Stand the casserole on the trivet. Put the lid on the cooker and bring to high (15 lb) pressure. Cook for 10 minutes. Reduce pressure quickly, fluff the rice and top with the raw fish, salt and pepper and parsley. Put on the lid and bring to high pressure. Cook for 5 minutes. Reduce pressure and serve.

Paupiettes of plaice au gratin

4 medium to large plaice fillets, skinned
salt and pepper
10 ml (2 tsp) lemon juice
50 g (2 oz) ham, finely chopped
75 g (3 oz) fresh breadcrumbs
75 g (3 oz) grated cheese
30 ml (2 tbsp) chopped parsley
4 large firm tomatoes
25 g (1 oz) butter

Put the fish fillets, skinned side uppermost, on a board. Sprinkle them with salt, pepper and a little lemon juice. Roll up from the tail end and stand them in a buttered flameproof dish or casserole. Mix together the ham, half the crumbs and half the cheese and the parsley; season well. Using a sharp pointed knife, cut a round from the stalk end of each tomato, scoop out the flesh and strain the juice on to the breadcrumb mixture; mix well. Refill the tomatoes with the stuffing and stand them in a dish with the fish. Put a few pieces of butter (about half) on top and cover lightly with a piece of foil.

Put the trivet in the pressure cooker and pour in 300 ml (½ pint) water. Stand the dish on the trivet and put on the lid. Bring the cooker to high (15 lb) pressure. Cook for 5 minutes. Reduce pressure quickly. Remove the dish from the cooker and sprinkle the fish with the remaining cheese and crumbs. Dot with the rest of the butter and brown

under a hot grill. Small or sliced potatoes may be cooked and served at the same time with the paupiettes.

Haddock portugaise

2 medium-size onions, skinned and sliced
30 ml (2 tbsp) oil
450 g (1 lb) tomatoes, skinned and sliced
1 large clove of garlic, skinned and crushed
5 ml (1 level tsp) sugar
salt and pepper
60 ml (4 tbsp) dry white wine
4 fillets of haddock about 175 g (6 oz) each
450 g (1 lb) potatoes, peeled and sliced
350 g (12 oz) frozen French beans
25 g (1 oz) butter

Lightly fry the onions in the heated oil in a pan until just tender. Stir in the tomatoes, crushed garlic, sugar, and seasoning. Cook for about 2 minutes, stirring, then put the mixture in an ovenproof dish or casserole that will fit in the pressure cooker. Pour in the wine and arrange the folded fillets of fish on top. Sprinkle with more salt and pepper and cover with foil. Pour 300 ml (½ pint) water in the pressure cooker, put in the trivet and stand the fish dish on it.

Arrange the potatoes in a buttered dish or separator and put the beans in another vegetable separator. Sprinkle the vegetables with salt, and put them in the cooker. Put on the lid and bring to high (15 lb) pressure. Cook for 4–6 minutes, according to thickness of fish and dishes. Reduce pressure slowly. Transfer the vegetables to a serving dish, adding two or three knobs of butter. Serve at once with the haddock.

Haddock fillets au gratin

700 g (1 ½ lb) haddock, in 4 fillets
salt and pepper
25 g (1 oz) butter or margarine
45 ml (3 level tbsp) flour
150 ml (¼ pint) milk
5 ml (1 level tsp) made mustard
100 g (4 oz) grated mature cheese

Put the trivet in the pressure cooker and pour in 150 ml (¼ pint) water. Fold the fillets of fish, skin side inside, in half and put them on the trivet. Sprinkle with salt and pepper. Put on the lid and bring to high (15 lb) pressure. Cook for 4 minutes. Reduce pressure quickly. Carefully remove the fillets and put them in a flameproof flat dish; keep hot.

Strain off the liquid from the cooker and reserve. Melt the fat in a pan, stir in the flour and cook for a few minutes. Remove the pan from the heat, stir in the milk, then stir in the hot fish liquid. Return the pan to the heat, stirring until the sauce thickens and boils. Add the seasonings and three quarters of the cheese; mix well. Pour the sauce over the fish, sprinkle with the remaining cheese and brown under a hot grill.

Stuffed mackerel fillets

2 large mackerel, filleted

For the stuffing
6 gherkins
175 g (6 oz) cooking apple
75 g (3 oz) celery washed, trimmed and chopped
25 g (1 oz) butter or margarine
2.5 ml (½ level tsp) dried thyme
5 ml (1 tsp) vinegar
45 ml (3 level tbsp) fresh breadcrumbs
salt and pepper

For the sauce
150 ml (¼ pint) apple juice
5 ml (1 level tsp) arrowroot
5 ml (1 tsp) lemon juice

Chop two of the gherkins and make the others into fans for the garnish. Peel, core and chop the apples and fry them with the celery in the fat in a small pan until the apple is pulpy. Stir in the chopped gherkins, thyme, vinegar, breadcrumbs and seasoning and mix well. Put the fish fillets on a board and spread the stuffing over them, then fold them in half and put them in a greased ovenproof dish that will fit into the pressure cooker. Put the trivet in the pressure cooker, pour in 300 ml (½ pint) water and stand the fish on the trivet. Put on the lid and bring to high (15 lb) pressure. Cook for 5 minutes. Reduce pressure quickly.

Meanwhile heat the apple juice in a pan. Blend the arrowroot and lemon juice and pour in a little of the hot apple juice. Add mixture to the pan and reheat, stirring until it thickens and boils. Serve the mackerel with a little of the sauce spooned over it, garnish with the gherkin fans and serve the rest of the sauce separately.

Herrings in red wine

1 medium-size onion, skinned and sliced
2–3 sticks of celery, trimmed, washed and chopped
1 medium carrot, scraped and sliced
25 g (1 oz) butter or margarine
salt and pepper
bouquet garni
300 ml (½ pint) red wine
6 herrings, cleaned with heads, tails and fins removed
100g (4 oz) button mushrooms
12 shallots, skinned
15 ml (1 tbsp) chopped parsley

Lightly fry the vegetables in the fat in the uncovered cooker until just slightly browned. Add the seasoning and bouquet garni and pour in the wine. Carefully lower the trivet on to the vegetables and put the herrings on it. Sprinkle with salt and pepper. Put the mushrooms and shallots together in a vegetable separator, sprinkle them with salt and pepper and put the separator in the cooker. Put on the lid and bring to high (15 lb) pressure. Cook for 6 minutes. Reduce pressure

quickly. Remove the herrings, place them on the vegetables in a shallow casserole and pour the cooking liquid over them. Garnish with the mushrooms, shallots and parsley.

Devonshire cod

50 g (2 oz) butter or margarine
700 g (1½ lb) cod, skinned and cut into 7·5-cm (2-in) pieces
2 medium-size onions, skinned and sliced
2 leeks, sliced and washed
2 sticks of celery, washed, trimmed and chopped
2 medium potatoes, peeled and sliced
2 streaky bacon rashers, rinded and diced
4 medium tomatoes, skinned and sliced
bayleaf
1 clove of garlic, skinned and crushed
150 ml (¼ pint) cider
salt and pepper
60-g (2-oz) can of anchovy fillets, drained

Melt the fat in the uncovered cooker and lightly fry the fish. Remove the fish and fry the onions, leeks, celery, potatoes and bacon until they are lightly browned. Stir in the tomatoes, bayleaf, garlic and cider. Season lightly and put the fish on top. Put on the lid and bring to high (15 lb) pressure. Cook for 6 minutes. Reduce pressure quickly. Carefully remove the fish, spoon the vegetable mixture on to a hot dish and arrange the fish on top. Garnish with anchovies and serve with buttered crusty bread.

Red mullet with tomato sauce

4 red mullet about 125 g (5 oz) each, cleaned
1 medium-size onion, skinned and chopped
15 ml (1 tbsp) oil
1 clove of garlic, skinned and crushed
425-g (15-oz) can of tomatoes
15 ml (1 level tbsp) tomato paste
5 ml (1 level tsp) sugar
bayleaf
salt and pepper

For the marinade

60 ml (4 tbsp) oil
60 ml (4 tbsp) vinegar
1 shallot, skinned and finely chopped
3 peppercorns, crushed
1 small bayleaf

Put the fish in a dish with the oil, vinegar, shallot, peppercorns and bayleaf. Leave to marinade for about 1 hour, turning them now and again.

Meanwhile lightly fry the onion in the heated oil in the uncovered pressure cooker, stir in the garlic, tomatoes with juice, tomato paste, sugar, bayleaf, salt and pepper. Put on the lid and bring to high (15 lb) pressure. Cook for 5 minutes. Reduce the pressure quickly. Discard the bayleaf and sieve the sauce or purée it in an electric blender. Adjust the seasoning.

Drain the fish from the marinade and put it in a buttered ovenproof dish, pour over half the sauce and cover with greased foil. Rinse out the cooker. Put 300 ml (½ pint) water in the cooker, put in the trivet and stand the fish on it. Put on the lid and bring to high (15 lb) pressure. Cook for 5 minutes. Meanwhile reheat the rest of the sauce. Reduce pressure quickly. Serve with the remaining sauce handed separately.

Sole fillets Toledo

25 g (1 oz) butter
1 large onion, skinned and sliced
1 medium green pepper, seeded and sliced
175 g (6 oz) long grain rice
1 clove of garlic, skinned and crushed
400 ml (¾ pint) fish or chicken stock
salt and pepper
8 small sole fillets, trimmed and skinned
15 ml (1 tbsp) lemon juice
15 ml (1 tbsp) chopped parsley

Melt the butter in a pan and lightly fry the onion and pepper without browning. Remove the vegetables from the pan and put them in a casserole or ovenproof dish that will fit easily into the pressure cooker. Stir the rice into remaining fat in the pan and cook without browning until all the fat has been absorbed and the rice grains are transparent. Stir in the garlic, stock and seasoning. Then add these ingredients to the casserole and mix well.

Put the trivet in the pressure cooker and pour in 300 ml (½ pint) water. Stand the casserole on the trivet. Put on the lid and bring to high (15 lb) pressure. Cook for 10 minutes. Meanwhile spread the sole fillets on a board, skinned side uppermost, season and sprinkle with lemon juice. Fold each fillet in 3, place them in a piece of greased foil and make into a neat parcel. Reduce pressure in the cooker quickly. Fluff the rice, put in the fish and put on the lid. Bring to high (15 lb) pressure. Cook for a further 5 minutes. Reduce pressure quickly. Arrange the rice on a hot dish surrounded by the fish fillets. Sprinkle with parsley before serving.

Kedgeree

450 g (1 lb) smoked haddock
175 g (6 oz) long grain rice
400 ml (¾ pint) water
5 ml (1 level tsp) salt
2 eggs, unshelled
50 g (2 oz) butter
30 ml (2 tbsp) chopped parsley
salt and freshly ground pepper

Cut the haddock into two or three pieces. Put the trivet in the pressure cooker and pour in 300 ml (½ pint) water. Put the fish on the trivet. Grease an ovenproof dish or solid separator and put the washed rice in it with 400 ml (¾ pint) water and 5 ml (1 level tsp) salt. Put the eggs in another separator. Put the rice and eggs in the cooker. Put on the lid and bring to high (15 lb) pressure. Cook for 5 minutes. Reduce pressure slowly.

Take out the rice and fluff it up with a fork. Take out fish, remove the bones and flake the flesh. Shell the eggs and roughly chop them. Melt the butter in the drained and rinsed cooker, stir in the rice, fish, egg, parsley and plenty of seasoning. Reheat gently, uncovered, using a fork to stir now and again. Pile the kedgeree on to a hot dish and serve with buttered toast.

Fish pudding

450 g (1 lb) cod or whiting fillets, skinned and cut
    into 1-cm (½-in) pieces
100 g (4 oz) fresh white breadcrumbs
30 ml (2 tbsp) chopped parsley
10 ml (2 tsp) lemon juice
salt and pepper
2 eggs
50 g (2 oz) butter or margarine
300 ml (½ pint) milk
300 ml (½ pint) shrimp or egg sauce (see below)

Put the fish with the crumbs, parsley, lemon juice and plenty of seasoning in a bowl. Whisk the eggs in a separate bowl. Melt the fat in a small pan and heat the milk to nearly boiling point, then whisk them both into the egg; mix well and pour on to the fish mixture. Leave to soak for 2–3 minutes, then put in a 600-ml (1-pint) greased pudding basin or straight sided mould or soufflé dish. Put the trivet in the pressure cooker and pour in 300 ml (½ pint) water. Stand the pudding on the trivet and cover with foil. Put on the lid and bring to high (15 lb) pressure. Cook for 15 minutes. Reduce pressure slowly. Serve with shrimp or egg sauce.

Shrimp or egg sauce
Make 300 ml (½ pint) white sauce and stir in 50 g (2 oz) chopped, peeled shrimps or 2 chopped hardboiled eggs.

Moules marinière

2·2 litres (4 pints) mussels
1 medium-sized onion, skinned and chopped
2 cloves of garlic, skinned and crushed
1 stick of celery, washed, trimmed and chopped
bouquet garni
4 peppercorns
½ standard size bottle of dry white wine
50 g (2 oz) beurre manié (see page 32)
2 egg yolks
142-ml (¼-pint) carton of double cream
90 ml (6 tbsp) chopped parsley

Wash and scrub the mussels under running cold water and remove the beards. Discard any mussels with broken or open shells. Rinse well and leave to drain. Put the mussels in the pressure cooker (do not more than half fill – if necessary carry out process twice) with the vegetables, bouquet garni, peppercorns and wine. Put on the lid and bring to high (15 lb) pressure, then cook for 1 minute. Reduce pressure quickly. Strain the liquid into a bowl. Remove the top shells and put the mussels in a hot dish. Return the liquid to the cooker and heat uncovered to boiling point. Whisk in the beurre manié gradually until the liquid has thickened slightly. Blend together the egg yolks and cream. Adjust the seasoning and remove cooker from the heat. Stir in the egg and cream mixture; stir until the sauce thickens a little more. Pour the sauce over the mussels. Sprinkle with chopped parsley and serve immediately.

Beurre manié

Work 25 g (1 oz) butter and 25 g (1 oz) flour together until a smooth paste is formed.

Guide to cooking time for pressure cooking fish at high (15 lb) pressure

The times given in the table vary slightly according to the size and thickness of the fish, but experience will help you to judge the required time. When the fish is cooked, it changes from a transparent close texture to a white milky appearance with loose flakes which fall away from the bone easily.

Fish	Cutlets, steaks or fillets	Whole fish or pieces
Bass	steaks 3–4 minutes	small 5–6 minutes per 450 g (1 lb)
Bream	fillets 3–4 minutes	5–6 minutes per 450 g (1 lb)
Cod	steaks 3–4 minutes fillet 3–4 minutes	small whole 4 minutes per 450 g (1 lb)
Coley	fillet 4 minutes	
Eel (Conger)	steaks 5 minutes	piece 5 minutes per 450 g (1 lb)
Haddock (fresh)	fillet 3–4 minutes	piece 4 minutes per 450 g (1 lb)
(smoked)	fillets 3–5 minutes (according to size)	whole piece 5 minutes per 450 g (1 lb)
Hake	steaks 3–4 minutes	piece 4 minutes per 450 g (1 lb)
Halibut	steaks 5 minutes (according to size)	piece 5 minutes per 450 g (1 lb)
Herrings	flat fillets 3 minutes rolled fillets 5 minutes	whole 5–6 minutes
Kippers		3–4 minutes (according to size)
Mackerel	fillets 4–5 minutes	whole 5–6 minutes
Mullet (red)		small whole 4–5 minutes
Mussels		1–2 minutes
Plaice	fillets 2–3 minutes (according to size) thick or rolled fillets 4 minutes	small 3–4 minutes
Rock salmon	steaks or fillets 4 minutes	
Salmon	cutlets 6–8 minutes (according to thickness)	piece 6 minutes per 450 g (1 lb)
Seatrout		small whole 6 minutes per 450 g (1 lb)
Skate	pieces 4 minutes	
Sole	fillets 2–3 minutes (according to size) rolled 4 minutes	small whole 5 minutes thick pieces 6 minutes
Trout		small whole 5 minutes
Turbot	steaks 5 minutes fillets 4 minutes	piece 5 minutes per 450 g (1 lb)
Whiting	fillets 3 minutes	whole 4–5 minutes

FRESH VEGETABLES

Vegetables are an essential part of the diet as they provide necessary mineral salts, vitamins and roughage. The pressure cooker not only cooks them quickly but ensures that they retain their goodness and flavours by cooking them in the super heated steam, with no direct contact with the water.

All fresh root and green vegetables can be pressure cooked. (Frozen vegetables are dealt with on pages 113–115.) The vegetables should be as fresh as possible and prepared in the normal way. If several vegetables are to be cooked at the same time, the longest cooking ones should be cut in smaller pieces so that all the vegetables will be ready at the same time. As vegetables deteriorate quickly and lose their food value if left cut up or shredded for any length of time, it is best to prepare them near the required time. Pressure cooked vegetables seem to retain their mineral salts and flavour so well that they only require a light sprinkling of salt just before cooking. This is a great advantage for those on a low salt diet.

When vegetables are cooked in a pressure cooker, only a little liquid is required. The exact quantity depends upon the size and type of pressure cooker, so the manufacturer's instructions should be followed, but in most cases it is about 150 ml (¼ pint) to 300 ml (½ pint). The vegetables should not be cooked directly in the water, they are cooked in the steam from the water, therefore the trivet with or without vegetable separators should be used. Thus, even when several varieties of vegetables are cooked at the same time, each one retains its own flavour.

General instructions for pressure cooking fresh vegetables

1. Prepare the vegetables according to the type and variety (see pages 39–42). Cut vegetables of the same kind to about the same size.

2. Put the trivet in the cooker and pour in the correct amount of water.

3. Arrange the vegetables, either on the trivet or in the vegetable separators, and sprinkle sparingly with salt. The cooker should not be more than two thirds full, which will still allow the steam to circulate freely around the cooker. For vegetables requiring different times, reduce the pressure during the longest cooking item, then take off the lid and put the other vegetables in the cooker so that they are ready at the same time. But do not do this more than once; it is better to choose vegetables requiring the same cooking time instead.

4. Put on the lid and bring to high (15 lb) pressure and cook the vegetables to the required time.

5. Reduce pressure quickly, otherwise the vegetables will go on cooking. Remove the lid.

6. Serve the vegetables in a hot casserole or dish with melted butter, coated with sauce or sprinkled with parsley or chives, according to taste.

7. The remaining vegetable liquid can be used as stock for stews, soups or sauces.

Onion dumpling

4 medium-size onions, skinned
2 streaky bacon rashers, rinded and finely chopped
2 lamb's kidneys, skinned, cored and finely chopped
25 g (1 oz) butter or margarine
salt and freshly ground pepper

For the suet crust pastry
225 g (8 oz) self raising flour
pinch of salt
100 g (4 oz) shredded suet
about 150 ml (¼ pint) cold water

Put 150 ml (¼ pint) water into the pressure cooker and put in the trivet. Stand the onions on the trivet and sprinkle with a little salt. Put on the lid and bring to high (15 lb) pressure. Cook for 4–5 minutes (depending on size, but undercook rather than overcook). Reduce pressure quickly. Remove onions from the cooker. Carefully remove the centre from each onion and chop it, leaving the outside whole.

Lightly fry the bacon and kidneys in the fat in a small pan. Remove the pan from the heat and stir in the chopped onion; season well.

Make the suet crust pastry by mixing dry ingredients with enough water to make a soft dough. Knead the dough on a floured surface and divide it into four; roll each piece into a round large enough to enclose an onion. Stand an onion on each pastry round and fill the centre of each onion with stuffing. Damp the pastry edges and draw them together to enclose the onions. Stand each dumpling on a piece of greased foil and fold lightly round each dumpling, leaving space for expansion. Put 600 ml (1 pint) water into the cooker, put the dumplings in a separator or on the trivet. Put on the lid and steam over low heat for 10 minutes without the weight. Then bring the cooker to low (5 lb) pressure. Cook for 20 minutes. Reduce pressure slowly. Serve the dumplings with gravy.

Stuffed peppers

1 large onion, skinned and chopped
25 g (1 oz) butter or bacon fat
75 g (3 oz) long grain rice
50 g (2 oz) cooked ham or bacon, minced or finely chopped
50 g (2 oz) grated mature cheese
salt
freshly ground pepper
4 medium-size red or green peppers, washed

Lightly fry the onion in the fat in a small pan. Cook the rice (see page 76), and drain it well, then mix it

Stuffed peppers

with the onion. Stir in the chopped ham and grated cheese. Season well with salt and pepper. Cut the tops from the stalk end of each pepper and remove all the seeds; keep the tops for lids. Stuff each pepper with the savoury rice mixture and put on the lids. Stand the stuffed peppers in an ovenproof dish or on a flat vegetable separator. Sprinkle lightly with salt. Put 300 ml (½ pint) water in the pressure cooker and put in the trivet. Place the peppers in the cooker and put on the lid. Bring to high (15 lb) pressure. Cook for about 5 minutes. Reduce pressure quickly. Put the peppers on a serving dish and serve with a well flavoured gravy.

Savoury marrow with tomato sauce

1 dumpy marrow not longer than 20 cm (8 in) for a 4·5 litre (8 pint) pressure cooker
1 medium-size onion, skinned and chopped
15 ml (1 tbsp) oil
175 g (6 oz) raw minced beef
50 g (2 oz) mushrooms, finely chopped
60 ml (4 level tbsp) fresh breadcrumbs
2·5 ml (½ level tsp) mixed herbs
salt and pepper
fresh tomato sauce (see page 81)

Peel the marrow and trim off each end. Cut in half lengthways and remove the seeds. Put 300 ml (½ pint) water in the pressure cooker, put in the marrow and sprinkle lightly with salt. Put on the lid and bring to high (15 lb) pressure. Cook for 1 minute, then reduce the pressure quickly. Carefully remove the marrow halves and put one half on a piece of buttered foil.

Fry the onion in oil in a pan until it is just cooked, then stir in the minced beef and continue cooking until it has just changed colour. Add the mushrooms and cook for a few more minutes. Remove the cooker from heat and stir in the breadcrumbs, and herbs. Season well. Pile the mixture into the marrow half on the foil and then put the other half on top. Fold the foil to enclose the marrow and secure the ends.

Make up the water in the cooker to 300 ml (½ pint) water, if necessary. Put in the trivet and stand the marrow on it. Bring to high (15 lb) pressure.

Cook for 12 minutes. Reduce pressure quickly. Remove the marrow, carefully unfold the foil and roll the marrow on to a hot dish and keep it hot. Make the sauce in the cooker (see page 81) and serve it with the stuffed marrow.

Sliced potatoes au gratin

450 g (1 lb) old potatoes, peeled and thinly sliced
1 medium-size onion, skinned and sliced
150 ml (¼ pint) milk
150 ml (¼ pint) water
1 clove of garlic, skinned and crushed
salt
freshly ground pepper
100 g (4 oz) cooked ham or bacon, chopped
100 g (4 oz) mature cheese, grated
30 ml (2 tbsp) chopped parsley
butter

Put the sliced potatoes and onion in the pressure cooker without the trivet and pour on the milk and water. Add the garlic and seasoning. Put on the lid and bring to high (15 lb) pressure. Cook for 5 minutes. Reduce pressure quickly. Using a draining spoon, remove the potatoes and onion. Reserve the liquid. Layer them in a warm flameproof dish with the ham and cheese, with a sprinkling of parsley on each layer, pour over liquid from the cooker; top with a generous layer of cheese. Heat grill and cook until golden brown.

Cauliflower and bacon cheese

1 medium-size cauliflower
100 g (4 oz) streaky bacon rashers, rinded
salt
40 g (1½ oz) butter or margarine
45 ml (3 level tbsp) flour
150 ml (¼ pint) milk
100 g (4 oz) mature cheese, grated
2·5 ml (½ level tsp) made mustard
freshly ground pepper

Break the cauliflower into florets and wash. Cut the bacon in 2·5-cm (1-in) pieces and fry them gently in a pan until the fat runs out, then brown slightly. Remove bacon from the pan and run off the fat.

Put the trivet in the pressure cooker and pour in 300 ml (½ pint) water. Put the cauliflower florets

Sliced potatoes au gratin

into a separator, sprinkle with salt and put into the pressure cooker. Put on the lid and bring to high (15 lb) pressure. Cook for 3–4 minutes. Reduce pressure quickly. Place the cauliflower with the bacon in a hot ovenproof dish and keep it warm. Reserve 150 ml (¼ pint) of the vegetable stock to use in the sauce. Melt the fat in a pan over a gentle heat and stir in the flour, cook for 2–3 minutes. Remove pan from the heat and stir in the milk and stock, mix well and return to the heat, stirring until the sauce boils and thickens. Then stir in half the cheese, the mustard and seasoning and pour the sauce over the cauliflower. Sprinkle with the remaining cheese and brown under a hot grill.

Chicory with ham au gratin

4 chicory heads, washed
4 thin slices of ham
Dijon mustard
25 g (1 oz) butter or margarine
1 medium-size onion, skinned and chopped
1 clove of garlic, skinned and crushed
198-g (7-oz) can of tomatoes
salt and pepper
150 ml (¼ pint) stock
bouquet garni
100 g (4 oz) mature cheese, grated
25 g (1 oz) browned breadcrumbs

Put the trivet in the pressure cooker and pour in 300 ml (½ pint) water. Remove outer leaves from chicory, if necessary, and put the heads on the trivet; sprinkle lightly with salt. Put on the lid and bring to high (15 lb) pressure. Cook for about 5 minutes. Reduce pressure quickly. Remove the chicory from the cooker and drain off the liquid. Rinse out the cooker to use again.

Spread each slice of ham with a little mustard and wrap a slice around each head of chicory. Arrange chicory in an ovenproof dish and keep it hot. Melt the fat in the uncovered cooker and gently fry the onion until just transparent; stir in the garlic, tomatoes with the juice, the stock, and seasoning. Put on the lid and bring to high (15 lb) pressure. Cook for 3 minutes. Reduce pressure quickly. Remove the bouquet garni. Sieve the sauce or purée it in an electric blender. Reheat and stir in three quarters of the cheese. Adjust seasoning and pour the sauce over the chicory. Sprinkle with the crumbs and remaining cheese and brown under a hot grill.

Potato and liver casserole

100g (4 oz) lamb's liver, skinned and diced
15 ml (1 level tbsp) seasoned flour
15 ml (1 tbsp) oil
1 medium-size onion, skinned and chopped
1 small clove of garlic, skinned and crushed
198-g (7-oz) can of tomatoes
1·25 ml (¼ level tsp) mixed herbs
100 g (4 oz) cooked shoulder ham or cold bacon, minced
salt and pepper
pinch of sugar
4–6 medium-size potatoes, peeled and thinly sliced
30 ml (2 tbsp) single cream
15 ml (1 level tbsp) chopped chives

Toss the liver in the seasoned flour. Heat the oil in the uncovered pressure cooker and lightly fry until it is just firm. Then remove it from the cooker. Put in the onion and garlic and fry until just transparent. Drain juices from tomatoes into the cooker. Cut up the tomatoes, and add with the herbs. Stir in the liver and ham. Put contents of cooker in a casserole which will fit in the cooker. Adjust

seasoning with salt, pepper and pinch of sugar. Cover with foil.

Rinse out the cooker and pour in 300 ml (½ pint) water. Put in the trivet, place the potatoes on it and sprinkle with a little salt. Put on the lid and bring to high (15 lb) pressure. Cook for 3 minutes. Reduce pressure quickly. Remove the potatoes from the cooker and arrange them on top of the meat in the casserole, spoon over the cream. Place the casserole in the cooker, put on the lid and bring to high (15 lb) pressure. Cook for 5 minutes. Reduce pressure quickly. Remove casserole, sprinkle chopped chives over the potatoes and serve.

Cabbage stuffed with bacon

1 white cabbage 1·4 kg (3 lb)
salt
225 g (8 oz) gammon slipper or trimmed bacon chops
15 ml (1 tbsp) oil
439-g (15½-oz) can of whole chestnuts, drained
freshly ground black pepper
300 ml (½ pint) chicken stock
30 ml (2 level tbsp) cornflour

Trim the cabbage and discard discoloured leaves. Put 300 ml (½ pint) water in the pressure cooker, put in trivet and stand the cabbage on it; sprinkle with salt. Put on the lid and bring to high (15 lb) pressure. Cook for 4 minutes. Reduce pressure quickly. Take out the cabbage and drain well. Scoop the inside from the cabbage, discarding the hard core, and leave the outer shell intact. Finely shred about 225 g (8 oz) of the inside part of the cabbage.

Cut the bacon into thin strips and fry it gently in hot oil in a large frying pan for about 10 minutes, add the shredded cabbage and continue cooking for 5 minutes. Stir in the chestnuts and season to taste. Stuff this mixture into the cabbage, then wrap the cabbage in a large piece of greased foil.

Pour another 300 ml (½ pint) water into the cooker and stand the cabbage on the trivet. Put on the lid and bring to high (15 lb) pressure. Cook for 30 minutes. Reduce the pressure quickly. Place the cabbage in a hot dish and keep it warm. Remove the trivet from the cooker and pour off some of the stock, leaving about 300 ml (½ pint). Blend the cornflour with a little cold water, stir in a little hot stock, then add the mixture to the cooker and stir until the sauce thickens and boils. Pour the sauce round the stuffed cabbage.

Quick ratatouille

30 ml (2 tbsp) olive oil
25 g (1 oz) butter
1 small green pepper, seeded and sliced
1 small red pepper, seeded and sliced
1 aubergine, sliced
2–3 courgettes, trimmed and sliced
4 tomatoes, skinned and quartered
1 clove of garlic, skinned and crushed
bayleaf
pinch of mixed herbs
salt
freshly ground pepper

Heat the oil and butter in a pan and lightly fry all the prepared vegetables for about 4 minutes. Add the garlic, herbs and seasoning. Put in a solid separator or ovenproof dish and cover with foil. Put the trivet in the pressure cooker, and pour in 300 ml (½ pint) water. Stand the dish on the trivet in the cooker. Put on the lid and bring to high (15 lb) pressure. Cook for 8 minutes. Reduce pressure quickly. Remove the ratatouille and adjust seasoning. Serve the vegetable stew hot with meat or cold as a summer salad.

Cabbage parcels

8 large Savoy cabbage leaves
5 ml (1 level tsp) salt
1 large onion, skinned and chopped
100 g (4 oz) mushrooms chopped
50 g (2 oz) butter or margarine
100 g (4 oz) cooked rice
50 g (2 oz) mature cheese, grated
salt and pepper
5 ml (1 level tsp) sugar
300 ml (½ pint) tomato juice

Put 300 ml (½ pint) water in the pressure cooker with the trivet. Wash the cabbage leaves and remove any hard stalk but keep the leaves whole.

Put the leaves in the cooker, sprinkle them with salt and put on the lid. Bring to high (15 lb) pressure. Cook for 3 minutes. Reduce pressure quickly. Carefully remove the leaves from the cooker and spread them on a board.

Meanwhile fry the onion and mushrooms in the fat in a frying pan until tender. Stir in the rice and cheese and season well. Divide the stuffing mixture between the eight leaves and fold them into parcels. Arrange the cabbage parcels in an ovenproof dish and sprinkle them with a little seasoning. Stir the sugar into the tomato juice and pour the juice over the cabbage parcels. Make sure there is still about 300 ml (½ pint) water in the cooker. Cover the dish with foil and stand it on the trivet in the cooker. Put on the lid and bring to high (15 lb) pressure. Cook for 10 minutes. Reduce pressure slowly.

Pork and spiced cabbage

225 g (8 oz) pickled salt pork, soaked for about 2 hours
1 medium-size onion, skinned and chopped
½ red cabbage about 450 g (1 lb)
2 medium-size cooking apples, peeled and cored
10 ml (2 level tsp) brown sugar
salt
6 peppercorns, crushed
2·5 ml (½ level tsp) ground cinnamon
pinch of nutmeg
75 ml (5 tbsp) stock or water
75 ml (5 tbsp) red wine vinegar
25 g (1 oz) raisins

Dice the pork into 1-cm (½-in) pieces. Heat it gently in the uncovered pressure cooker until the fat runs out, then brown it slightly. Remove the meat from the cooker and lightly fry the onion until transparent. Remove the thick stalk or core from the cabbage and cut the leaves into 1-cm (½-in) slices. Dice the apples. Fry the cabbage and apple in the remaining fat in the cooker for a few minutes. Then stir in the pork with the rest of the ingredients. Put on the lid and bring to high (15 lb) pressure. Cook for 5 minutes. Reduce pressure quickly. Mix well and adjust seasoning before serving.

Casserole of vegetables

175 g (6 oz) carrots, scraped and sliced
2–3 onions, skinned and sliced
2 stalks of celery, trimmed and chopped
small piece of swede, peeled and diced
300 ml (½ pint) chicken stock
15 ml (1 level tbsp) tomato paste
bouquet garni
salt
freshly ground pepper
175 g (6 oz) frozen broad beans
175 g (6 oz) frozen peas
15 ml (1 level tbsp) cornflour

Lightly fry the fresh vegetables in the oil in the uncovered cooker for about 5 minutes. Pour in the stock, add the tomato paste and bouquet garni; season well. Put on the lid and bring to high (15 lb) pressure. Cook for 3 minutes. Then reduce pressure quickly and add frozen vegetables, broken up if they are not free flowing. Put on the lid and bring back to high (15 lb) pressure. Cook for 3 more minutes. Reduce pressure quickly. Remove the bouquet garni. Blend the cornflour to a paste with a little cold water, then stir in a little of the hot liquid. Add the mixture to the cooker and stir over the heat until the stewed vegetables have thickened and boiled. Adjust seasoning. Serve with sliced beef or lamb.

Cheese and celery custard

1 small head of celery, washed and diced
1 medium-size onion, skinned and chopped
salt
150 ml (¼ pint) milk
142-ml (5 fl oz) carton of single cream
2 eggs
100 g (4 oz) mature cheese, grated
freshly ground pepper
50 g (2 oz) streaky bacon, rinded

Put the celery and onion in a vegetable separator and sprinkle lightly with salt. Put 300 ml (½ pint) water in the pressure cooker, put in the trivet and stand the vegetables on it. Put on the lid and bring to high (15 lb) pressure. Cook for 5 minutes. Reduce pressure quickly. Turn vegetables into a 15-cm (6-in) soufflé dish. Warm the milk and the cream together almost to boiling point and whisk into the eggs. Mix well and stir in the grated cheese. Season with a little salt and freshly ground pepper. Pour the egg mixture over the celery, cover with foil and place the dish in the cooker. Put on the lid and bring to high (15 lb) pressure. Cook for about 8 minutes (depending on the thickness of the dish). Meanwhile grill the bacon rashers until brown and crisp, then crumble them. Reduce pressure slowly. Sprinkle the cheese and celery custard with the bacon and serve with hot buttered toast.

Spiced vegetables

(See colour picture facing page 49)

If wished, 15 ml (1 level tbsp) curry powder may be substituted for the cummin, coriander, turmeric and ginger in this recipe.

5 ml (1 level tsp) cummin powder
5 ml (1 level tsp) ground coriander
5 ml (1 level tsp) ground turmeric
2·5 ml (½ level tsp) ground ginger
30 ml (2 tbsp) oil
1 small cooking apple
450 g (1 lb) cauliflower, in florets
225 g (8 oz) carrots, scraped and sliced
225 g (8 oz) onions, skinned and sliced
1 clove of garlic, skinned and crushed
5 ml (1 level tsp) salt
5 ml (1 level tsp) sugar
141-g (5-oz) carton of yoghurt

Mix the spices together and fry them in the oil in the uncovered pressure cooker for about 5 minutes. Meanwhile peel and chop the apple. Stir in the vegetables and cook for about 2 minutes, until well covered with oil and spices. Then stir in the garlic and apple and sprinkle with salt and sugar. Remove the vegetables from cooker and put them in a solid container or ovenproof dish. Rinse out the cooker and put in 300 ml (½ pint) water and the trivet. Stand the dish of vegetables on the trivet. Put on the lid and bring to high (15 lb) pressure. Cook for 10 minutes (allow extra time if a thick dish is used). Reduce pressure quickly and remove the vegetables. Stir in the yoghurt and serve with sliced meats or a cheese dish or something similar.

Vegetable casserole with cheese dumplings

225 g (8 oz) mushrooms, sliced
2 medium-size onions, skinned and sliced
225 g (8 oz) courgettes, sliced
50 g (2 oz) butter or margarine
salt and pepper
1 clove of garlic, skinned and crushed
300 ml (½ pint) tomato juice
5 ml (1 level tsp) sugar

For the cheese dumplings
100 g (4 oz) self raising flour
pinch of salt
50 g (2 oz) margarine
50 g (2 oz) mature cheese, grated
2·5 ml (½ level tsp) dry mustard
pepper
60 ml (4 tbsp) water

Lightly fry the prepared vegetables in the fat in the uncovered pressure cooker for about 4 minutes.

Sprinkle with salt and pepper and add the garlic. Spoon the mixture into a deep 15-cm (6-in) soufflé dish and pour in the tomato juice sprinkled with sugar. Rinse out the cooker. Put 600 ml (1 pint) water in the cooker with the trivet. Stand the vegetables on the trivet and cover lightly with foil. Put on the lid of the cooker and bring to high (15 lb) pressure. Cook for 8 minutes.

Meanwhile make the dumplings. Put the flour and salt in a bowl, rub in the margarine, add the cheese and seasoning, then mix to a soft dough with water. Form the dough into eight balls. Reduce the cooker pressure quickly. Bring contents of cooker to the boil and add the dumplings. Put on the lid, without the weight, and return the cooker to the heat. Adjust the heat so that the cooker emits a steady but gentle flow of steam for 3 minutes. Then put on the weight and increase the heat to bring to high (15 lb) pressure. Cook for a further 3 minutes. Reduce pressure slowly and serve at once.

Guide to cooking fresh vegetables in a pressure cooker

As the timing for vegetable cooking is so short, it is important to ensure that the vegetables are not overcooked. One extra minute of pressure cooking is equivalent to about 15 minutes of boiling. Therefore it is helpful to use a timer or stop watch to get the best results, starting the timing from the moment pressure is reached. A guide to pressure cooking fresh vegetables is given below but it should be remembered that the age, size, variety and freshness of the vegetables should also be taken into account when calculating the cooking time.

Vegetable	Preparation	Pressure cooking time at high (15 lb) pressure	Serving suggestions
Artichokes Jerusalem	Scrub and peel – keep in water with lemon juice or vinegar added, until required. Cut large ones in half.	*5–7 minutes*	With melted butter and sprinkled with parsley; with cheese or hollandaise sauce.
Asparagus	Choose stems of even thickness. Trim stalks to same size and tie into bundles. Stand them in vegetable separator or spread on a flat separator.	2–4 minutes, according to thickness	With melted butter, hollandaise sauce or mayonnaise.
Aubergines	Wash and slice.	5 minutes	With melted butter and chopped parsley.

Vegetable	Preparation	Pressure cooking time at high (15 lb) pressure	Serving suggestions
Beans, broad	Shell and put in vegetable separator.	4–5 minutes	With butter or parsley sauce.
French	Cut the tops and tails off, but leave whole.	3 minutes	With melted butter.
runner	String and slice, put in separator.	2–3 minutes	With melted butter.
Beetroot	Remove leaves or small roots but leave whole.	Add 600 ml (1 pint) water for small beet; 900 ml (1½ pints) water for medium; 1·1 litres (2 pints) water for large beet. 10–30 minutes according to size.	Hot with white sauce or hot horseradish sauce. Cold with French dressing or vinegar.
Broccoli purple or white sprouting	Wash and trim, discard discoloured leaves. Break large stalks in half.	3–4 minutes	Plain or buttered.
Brussels sprouts	Trim stalks and cut if large. Discard discoloured leaves. Put in separator.	3–4 minutes	Plain or buttered.
Cabbage, green	Trim and discard discoloured leaves and coarse stalks. Slice into 1-cm (½-in) shreds just before cooking.	3–4 minutes	Plain or buttered, or with chopped parsley and freshly ground pepper.
red	Trim and discard outer leaves. Shred into 1-cm (½-in) slices.	Add 30 ml (2 tbsp) vinegar to cooking water. 5 minutes	With grated nutmet and caraway seeds.
Carrots	Wash and scrape or peel, according to age. Young carrots are best left whole. Older carrots, sliced or halved or quartered.	Young carrots whole, 5–6 minutes. Sliced old carrots, 4–5 minutes. Whole old carrots, 6–8 minutes.	With butter and parsley.
Cauliflower	Trim off outer leaves and discard the coarse stalks. Cut a cross in stalk end with sharp knife; leave whole or break into florets. Put pieces in separator.	Whole cauliflower, 5–6 minutes. Florets, 3–4 minutes according to size.	Plain or butter or with white, cheese or parsley sauce.
Celeriac	Peel thickly and cut into 1-cm (½-in) slices or dice.	6–8 minutes depending on size and age.	Buttered; or with béchamel, cheese or hollandaise sauce.
Celery	Trim and cut off leafy ends. Cut into 5-cm (2-in) lengths, or leave in small whole hearts trimmed to about 15 cm (6 in).	Celery pieces, 3–4 minutes. Celery hearts, 6–7 minutes.	Plain or buttered; or coated with white or cheese sauce.

Vegetable	Preparation	Pressure cooking time at high (15 lb) pressure	Serving suggestions
Chicory	Trim a thin slice from base of head and remove dry outer leaves. Leave whole.	3–5 minutes according to thickness of head.	With melted butter, chopped parsley or paprika pepper.
Corn on the cob	Remove outer leaves and silky threads. Shorten stalks level with the corn.	3–5 minutes depending on thickness and size.	With melted butter.
Courgettes	Trim dry ends, leave whole or halve or slice. Put slices in separator.	Whole, 5 minutes. Cut, 2–3 minutes.	Tossed in butter or served cold with French dressing.
Fennel	Trim and wash. Remove feathery tops and outer leaves. Leave whole or halve.	Whole, 6–8 minutes. Halved, 5–6 minutes.	With melted butter; or white or cheese sauce.
Leeks	Remove coarse outer leaves and cut off tops and root. Split down the centre and wash thoroughly or cut into 5-cm (2-in) slices and wash well.	3–5 minutes depending on thickness.	With white or cheese sauce.
Marrow	Remove peel and seeds and cut into 4-cm (1½-in) slices, or leave in rings, or halve for stuffing.	Slices, 3–4 minutes. Halved, 4–5 minutes.	With white, cheese or parsley sauce.
Mushrooms, small button	Trim and wipe. Leave whole.	2–3 minutes	Tossed in butter or sprinkled with parsley.
Large flat	Trim, wipe and stuff.	3–4 minutes	
Onions	Skin and leave whole or skin and slice.	Whole, 5–10 minutes. Sliced, 3–4 minutes.	Topped with butter and parsley.
Parsnips	Peel and cut into quarters or dice. If centre core is very hard, remove it.	5–6 minutes depending on size and age.	With parsley sauce or butter and freshly ground pepper.
Peas	Shell and put in separator with sprig of mint.	Very young, 3 minutes. Garden peas, 3–4 minutes.	With butter and sprinkling of sugar.
Mange-tout	Trim ends and leave whole.	3 minutes	As above.
Peppers (capsicum), red or green	Remove centre stalk and seeds. Leave whole or cut into 1-cm (½-in) slices.	Whole stuffed, 5–8 minutes depending upon stuffing. Sliced, 3–4 minutes.	With a good rich gravy. Tossed in butter.

Vegetable	Preparation	Pressure cooking time at high (15 lb) pressure	Serving suggestions
Potatoes, new	Scrub or scrape or leave unscraped. Cook with sprig of mint.	Small whole, 5–7 minutes. Medium whole, 7–9 minutes.	Buttered and sprinkled with chopped chives, parsley or mint.
old	Scrub and peel, or leave unpeeled. Leave whole or cut into dice or slices.	Whole, 4–5 minutes depending upon size. Diced or sliced, 3–4 minutes.	Sprinkled with chopped chives or parsley; can be mashed or creamed.
Seakale	Wash well and trim to even lengths. Cut off root ends and tie into bundles.	4–5 minutes	With melted butter or hollandaise sauce.
Spinach	Wash well in several changes of water and discard thick stalks. Put in pressure cooker without trivet and with water clinging to leaves, sprinkle with a little salt.	Bring to pressure only	Drain well and serve with butter, freshly ground pepper and lemon juice.
Swedes	Peel thickly and cut into 1-cm (½-in) slices, or dice.	4–5 minutes depending on size.	Serve with butter and chopped parsley, or mash and serve sprinkled with parsley.
Turnip	Peel thickly and cut into 1-cm (½-in) slices, or dice.	4–5 minutes	Serve mashed with butter and chopped parsley.

POT ROASTING, BRAISING AND COOKING BOILING JOINTS

In this chapter specific numbers of servings are not given. This will vary considerably depending on whether the joint is carved entirely hot, half hot, and cold the next day, or only when cold.

Some of the cheaper joints of meat are ideal for pot roasting and braising and make a good alternative to the more expensive roasts. The normal cooking times can be reduced to between a quarter and a third when a pressure cooker is used, and joints or fowl that normally need long slow cooking can be tenderised in far less time.

Although a guide for the cooking times is included here, experience will help the cook to gauge the exact times required for various joints. Obviously the quality, cut, thickness, fat and bone are all factors that will determine the pressure cooking time. It is advisable not to attempt to cook too large a joint or bird in the pressure cooker; a 1·4–1·8 kg (3–4 lb) joint should be the maximum for a 4·5-litre (8-pint) model.

Pot roasting

This cooking method is very suitable for small compact joints, poultry and game. The meats may be boned and stuffed, but they should be well tied into shape. The joint is first browned all over in a little fat, the surplus is drained off and a little liquid is added to produce the steam which helps to cook the meat. The quantity of liquid depends on the size of the joint, but not less than 300 ml (½ pint) should be used, and 150 ml (¼ pint) should be added for every 450 g (1 lb) in excess of 900 g (2 lb). The meat stands on the trivet in the pressure cooker and vegetables can be cooked with the meat, according to the recipe. The pressure cooking time depends on weight and shape of joint (see chart on pages 54–55).

Braising

Small joints, poultry, chops, cutlets and individual portions are all suitable for braising. The meat is usually browned all over in a little fat. A mirepoix of vegetables is then fried in the fat until just brown. The trivet is not used as the meat is placed on top of the vegetables with seasonings and flavourings and liquid is added so that it just covers the vegetables. The pressure cooking time depends upon the weight and thickness of the meat (see chart on pages 54–55).

Cooking boiling joints

Pickled meats and old fowl are excellent when pressure cooked, although fresh meats may also be cooked to advantage by this method. The meat is put on the trivet in the pressure cooker, with the flavouring vegetables and herbs. Water is added according to the required cooking time (see chart). Pickled meats such as ham, pickled beef, tongue and pork should all be soaked in cold water at least 2 hours before cooking. Pickled meats require a little more cooking time than fresh meats.

Making stock

If you are buying boned and rolled joints from the butcher it is worth asking him for a few extra bones to add flavour to the stock. See page 17 for instructions for making stock.

Adding vegetables

When adding vegetables part of the way through the cooking, take into account the freshness and age of the vegetables, allowing a little longer for older ones. To help the time adjustment either leave the vegetables whole or in largish pieces. For quicker cooking cut up even smaller.

Boiled beef and carrots with herb dumplings

**Cooking time for beef:
13–15 minutes per 450 g (1 lb)**

As the meat is soaked in cold water for 24 hours before cooking, start the preparation for this recipe the day before it is needed.

**1 joint of pickled silverside of beef about 1·4 kg (3 lb)
3–4 onions, skinned
4–6 small carrots, pared
2–3 leeks, cut into 5-cm (2-in) lengths and washed
2 sticks of celery, washed and cut into 5-cm (2-in) lengths
bouquet garni
10 ml (2 level tsp) salt
4–6 peppercorns
1·1 litres (2 pints) water**

For the dumplings
**100 g (4 oz) self raising flour
pinch of salt
2·5 ml (½ level tsp) mixed herbs
50 g (2 oz) shredded suet
about 75 ml (5 tbsp) cold water**

Weigh the meat and calculate cooking time, taking into account the thickness of the joint. Soak the pickled meat in cold water for up to 24 hours.

Drain off the water from the meat and wash it well. Put the trivet in the pressure cooker and place the meat on it. Add a small amount of each vegetable, the bouquet garni, salt, peppercorns and water. Put on the lid and bring to high (15 lb) pressure, then cook for about 45 minutes (according to weight and thickness of the meat).

Meanwhile make the dumplings. Mix all the dry ingredients to a soft dough with about 75 ml (5 tbsp) cold water. Form the dough into eight balls. Five minutes before the end of the calculated cooking time, reduce pressure quickly and put in the remaining vegetables. Return the cooker to the heat, bring contents to the boil, and add the dumplings. Put on the lid and allow the cooker to steam gently for 3 minutes without the weight. Then put on the weight and bring to high (15 lb)

pressure. Then cook for 5 minutes. Reduce pressure quickly. Slice the beef and serve with the vegetables and dumplings.

Boiled lamb with caper sauce

**Cooking time for lamb:
10–12 minutes per 450 g (1 lb)**

**1 joint of best end of neck of lamb about 800 g–1 kg (1¾–2 ¼ lb)
10 ml (2 level tsp) salt
700 ml (1 ¼ pints) cold water
3–4 small onions, skinned
3–4 carrots, pared and quartered
1–2 sticks of celery, washed and halved
25 g (1 oz) butter or margarine
45 ml (3 level tbsp) flour
150 ml (¼ pint) milk
30 ml (2 tbsp) capers
10 ml (2 tsp) vinegar from capers bottle
pepper**

Trim the joint, weigh it and calculate cooking time, taking into account the thickness of the joint.

Put the trivet in the pressure cooker and put the trimmed joint on it. Sprinkle in the salt and pour on the water. Bring to the boil uncovered and remove any scum. Add a small amount of each vegetable, cover with the lid and bring to high (15 lb) pressure. Cook for about 18–30 minutes (according to weight and thickness of the joint). Five minutes before the end of the calculated cooking time, reduce pressure quickly and add the rest of the vegetables. Bring to high (15 lb) pressure again and cook for 5 minutes. Reduce pressure quickly. Place the meat on a serving dish and surround with the vegetables. Keep the meat hot. Strain the stock to use for the sauce.

Melt the fat in a pan and stir in the flour. Cook for 2–3 minutes, remove from heat and gradually stir in 300 ml (½ pint) of the hot lamb stock and the milk. Return pan to the heat and bring to the boil, stirring until the sauce thickens. Stir in the capers with 10 ml (2 tsp) vinegar. Adjust seasoning and serve with the meat.

Pickled pork with pease pudding

Cooking time for pork:
about 14 minutes per 450 g (1 lb)

*The pork for this dish needs to soak for about 12
hours, so start the preparation the day before the
dish is needed.*

1 joint of pickled streaky pork weighing about
    1 kg (2 ¼ lb)
225 g (8 oz) split peas
1 onion, skinned and quartered
bayleaf
4–6 peppercorns
600 ml (1 pint) water
25 g (1 oz) butter
salt and pepper
1 egg, beaten
chopped parsley

Weigh the pork and calculate cooking time, taking
into account the thickness of the joint. Soak the
pork in cold water for about 12 hours.

    Wash the peas, pour over boiling water to
cover and leave to soak for at least 1 hour. Drain
off the water and put the peas in a vegetable
separator covered with foil. Put the pork in the
pressure cooker with the onion, bayleaf and
peppercorns. Pour in the measured water and
put in the peas. Put on the lid and bring to high
(15 lb) pressure. Cook for 20 minutes. Reduce
pressure quickly. Remove the peas. Bring the
cooker to high (15 lb) pressure again and cook for
about 10 more minutes (depending on the weight
and thickness of the joint).

    Meanwhile mash or purée the cooked peas
through a wire sieve or in an electric blender. Melt
the butter in a small saucepan and stir in the peas.
Remove the pan from the heat, adjust seasoning
and beat in the egg. Reheat for a few minutes, then
pile the peas into a hot dish and sprinkle with
chopped parsley. Reduce the pressure in the
cooker quickly. Slice the meat and serve with the
pease pudding.

    Parsnips make an excellent accompaniment to
this dish. They can be added during the final
cooking of the meat.

Braised breast of veal

Cooking time for veal:
10–12 minutes per 450 g (1 lb)

900 g (2 lb) piece breast of veal, boned weight
    about 700 g (1 ½ lb)
100 g (4 oz) streaky bacon, rinded, diced and fried
30 ml (2 tbsp) oil
4 medium-size onions, skinned and quartered
225 g (8 oz) button mushrooms, washed
400 ml (¾ pint) stock or water
salt and pepper
bouquet garni

For the stuffing
100 g (4 oz) fresh white breadcrumbs
5 ml (1 level tsp) grated lemon rind
5 ml (1 level tsp) dried thyme
30 ml (2 tbsp) chopped parsley
salt and pepper
30 ml (2 tbsp) melted butter
1 egg

Spread the meat on a chopping board skin side
down, trim off the tapered end and shape into an
oblong. Sprinkle the bacon over the meat. Mix
together the ingredients for the stuffing, using the
butter and egg to bind it. Spread the stuffing on the
meat, roll up the meat and tie or sew it into a neat
shape.

    Weigh the prepared meat and calculate cook-
ing time, taking into account the thickness of the
joint. Brown the joint in the hot oil in the
uncovered pressure cooker and remove when
browned. Fry the onions and mushrooms until
brown. Pour in the stock just to cover the
vegetables, add the seasoning, bouquet garni and
the meat and any veal bones. Put on the lid, bring
to high (15 lb) pressure, then cook for about 20
minutes (according to stuffed weight and thickness). Reduce pressure quickly. Remove the bones
and bouquet garni. Serve vegetables and sliced
meat on a hot dish. Serve gravy separately.

Boiled bacon

Cooking time for bacon:
12–14 minutes per 450 g (1 lb)

1 piece of back, gammon or collar bacon, about
   1·3 kg (3 lb)
2 onions, skinned and quartered
2 carrots, scraped and quartered
bayleaf
4 peppercorns
browned breadcrumbs (if serving cold)

Weigh the bacon and calculate cooking time,
taking into account the thickness of the joint.

If using unsmoked bacon, first place it in the
open pressure cooker, cover with water, bring to
the boil, then drain away water. If using smoked
bacon, soak it for up to 4 hours in cold water.

Then place the bacon in the pressure cooker,
skin side down, add cold water so that it comes half
way up the bacon joint. Add onion, carrots,
bayleaf and peppercorns. Bring to the boil,
skimming off any scum that forms. Put lid on
cooker and bring up to high (15 lb) pressure. Cook
for about 40 minutes (according to weight and
thickness of the joint).

To serve the bacon hot, reduce pressure
quickly. Remove the joint from the cooker and
skin it. Serve with parsley sauce.

To serve the bacon cold, reduce pressure
slowly. Remove the joint from pressure cooker
and skin it. Press browned breadcrumbs into the
fat and leave it to cool.

Braised bacon

Cooking time for bacon:
12–14 minutes per 450 g (1 lb)

1·4 kg (3 lb) piece of collar or boned and rolled
   forehock of bacon; boned weight about 1·1 kg
   (2½ lb)
2 medium-size onions, skinned and quartered
4 carrots, scraped and sliced
½ small turnip, peeled and sliced
2 sticks of celery, washed and sliced
25 g (1 oz) butter or margarine
400 ml (¾ pint) stock
pepper; bouquet garni
15 ml (1 level tbsp) flour, blended with cold water

Soak the bacon for several hours before cooking.
Weigh the bacon and calculate cooking time,
taking into account the thickness of the joint.

Put the bacon on the trivet in the pressure
cooker, pour in 300 ml (½ pint) cold water. Put on
the lid and bring to high (15 lb) pressure. Cook for
10 minutes. Reduce pressure quickly. Remove the
joint and pour off liquid. If the liquid is very salty
discard it, if it is not use it as stock for further
cooking.

Lightly fry the vegetables in the fat until well
browned, pour in enough stock just to cover,
about 400 ml (¾ pint). Sprinkle with pepper and
add the bouquet garni. Put the bacon on top of the
vegetables. Put on the lid and bring to high (15 lb)
pressure. Cook for about 30 minutes (according to
weight and thickness of the joint). Reduce pressure quickly. Remove the bacon and vegetables
and take off the bacon rind. Add a little of the hot
liquid to the flour mixture, then stir it into the
liquid in the cooker and bring to the boil, stirring
until it has thickened. Serve the sliced bacon with
the vegetables. Hand the gravy separately. Alternatively, serve with Cumberland sauce.

Braised brisket

Cooking time for beef:
about 15 minutes per 450 g (1 lb)

*The meat is marinated for about 24 hours, so start
the preparation the day before it is to be cooked.*

1·4 kg (3 lb) joint of brisket of beef, boned and
   rolled; boned weight about 1·1 kg (2½ lb)
30 ml (2 tbsp) oil
2 large onions, skinned and quartered
2 large carrots, pared and sliced
2 sticks celery, washed and chopped
4 tomatoes, skinned and quartered
about 300 ml (½ pint) stock
30 ml (2 level tbsp) flour

For the marinade
150 ml (¼ pint) red wine
30 ml (2 tbsp) vinegar
15 ml (1 tbsp) oil
1 clove of garlic, skinned and crushed
5 ml (1 tsp) dried mixed herbs
1 bayleaf
salt and pepper

Weigh the meat and calculate cooking time, taking into account the thickness of the joint.

Stand the wiped joint in a deep dish. Mix together the marinade ingredients and pour them over the meat. Leave to steep for up to 24 hours, basting frequently.

Drain the marinade off the meat and keep it to use later. Wipe the joint and fry it until well browned in the hot oil in the uncovered pressure cooker. Remove the meat and fry the onions, carrots and celery until brown. Drain off any excess fat, then add the tomatoes. Pour in the marinade, made up to 400 ml (¾ pint) with stock. Stand the meat on the vegetables and put on the lid. Bring to high (15 lb) pressure, then cook for about 40 minutes. Reduce pressure quickly. Put the meat and vegetables on a serving dish. Return the cooking liquid to the heat. Blend the flour to a smooth cream with a little cold water, stir in a little of the hot liquid, then add mixture to the cooker; bring to the boil, stirring until the gravy thickens. Serve gravy separately. Horse-radish cream may also be served.

Braised pheasant with chestnuts

Cooking time for pheasant:
6–8 minutes per 450 g (1 lb)

1 young pheasant about 700 g (1½ lb) drawn and trussed
450 g (1 lb) whole chestnuts
15 ml (1 level tbsp) seasoned flour
50 g (2 oz) butter
8 small whole onions, skinned
2 medium-size onions, skinned and sliced
100 g (4 oz) ham or bacon, diced
100 g (4 oz) mushrooms, sliced
150 ml (¼ pint) Burgundy
400 ml (¾ pint) game stock (from giblets)
salt and pepper
bayleaf
15 ml (1 tbsp) chopped parsley
25 g (1 oz) beurre manié (see page 32)

Weigh the pheasant and calculate cooking time.

Put the chestnuts in the pressure cooker, cover with water, put on the lid and bring to high (15 lb) pressure. Cook for 2 minutes. Reduce pressure

quickly. Peel the chestnuts. Rinse out the cooker and fry the pheasant, dusted with the flour, in the hot butter until well browned. Remove pheasant from cooker and brown the small whole onions and chestnuts. Remove these from the cooker and fry the sliced onions, ham and mushrooms. Drain off excess fat, pour in the wine and stock and add the seasoning and bayleaf. Place the pheasant on the vegetables and ham in the cooker. Cover with the lid and bring to high (15 lb) pressure. Cook for about 12 minutes (according to weight). Five minutes before the end of the calculated cooking time, reduce pressure quickly and add the whole onions and chestnuts. Bring to high (15 lb) pressure again, and cook for a further 5 minutes. Reduce pressure quickly. Put the pheasant on a serving dish, arrange the vegetables round it and sprinkle with parsley. Discard the bayleaf. Return the cooking liquid to the heat and gradually whisk in the beurre manié, stirring until the gravy thickens and comes to the boil. Adjust seasoning and serve sauce separately.

Chicken with mushroom cream sauce

Cooking time for chicken:
6–8 minutes per 450 g (1 lb)

1 oven ready chicken about 1·5 kg (3½ lb) with giblets
15 ml (1 tbsp) lemon juice
1 medium-size onion, skinned
3–4 cloves
2 carrots, pared and quartered
bouquet garni
600 ml (1 pint) water
salt and pepper
175 g (6 oz) button mushrooms
50 g (2 oz) butter
30 g (2 level tbsp) flour
30 ml (2 tbsp) cream

Weigh the chicken and calculate cooking time.

Truss the bird into a neat shape and rub it all over with lemon juice. Put the trivet in the pressure cooker and put in the chicken, giblets, the onion stuck with the cloves, carrots and bouquet garni. Pour on the water and season. Cover with the lid and bring to high (15 lb) pressure. Cook for about 30 minutes (according to the weight). Reduce pressure quickly. Put the chicken on a serving dish with vegetables; keep hot. Strain the stock into a basin and skim off fat. Slice the mushrooms and lightly fry them in 25 g (1 oz) butter in another pan. Remove mushrooms from the pan and rinse out pan. Melt remaining butter in the pan. Stir in the flour and cook for a few minutes. Remove from the heat and gradually stir in 400 ml (¾ pint) skimmed chicken stock. Return sauce to the heat and bring to the boil. Adjust seasoning and lastly stir in the mushrooms and cream. Serve the sauce separately.

Chicken with tarragon sauce

Cooking time for chicken:
6–8 minutes per 450 g (1 lb)

This is a delicious dish to serve cold in the summer.

1 oven ready chicken about 1·4 kg (3 lb)
giblets
5 ml (1 level tsp) salt
a good shake of freshly ground pepper
25 g (1 oz) butter
a few fresh tarragon leaves, chopped
15 ml (1 tbsp) lemon juice
1 medium-size onion, skinned
bayleaf
600 ml (1 pint) water
3 egg yolks
142-ml (¼-pint) carton of double cream
30 ml (2 tbsp) white wine
lemon wedges
extra tarragon leaves for garnish

Weigh the chicken and calculate cooking time.

Mash the salt and pepper with the butter and chopped tarragon leaves. Rub the outside of the chicken with the lemon juice and put the butter mixture inside. Put the trivet in the pressure cooker and stand chicken and giblets on it. Add onion, bayleaf and tarragon stalks, pour on the water and put on the lid. Bring to high (15 lb) pressure and cook for about 20 minutes (according to weight). Reduce pressure quickly. Lift out the bird. Put in a deep dish. Strain the stock, measure 400 ml (¾ pint) into a pan and heat. Whisk together the egg yolks, cream and white wine. Remove stock from

the heat, stir in the egg and cream mixture and continue to heat very gently, stirring constantly until it thickens, but do not allow it to boil. Adjust the seasoning and pour the sauce over the whole chicken. Leave to get cold in the sauce. Carve and serve on a dish, garnished with lemon wedges and tarragon leaves.

Pressed pickled tongue

Cooking time for tongue:
15 minutes per 450 g (1 lb)

As the tongue has to be soaked overnight, start the preparation the day before the dish is needed.

1 pickled ox tongue about 1·4 kg (3 lb)
2 onions, skinned and quartered
2 carrots, pared and quartered
2 sticks of celery, washed and sliced
4–6 peppercorns
bouquet garni
about 1·7 litres (3 pints) cold water
15 ml (3 level tsp) gelatine

Weigh the tongue and calculate cooking time. Soak the tongue overnight in cold water.

Put the trivet in the pressure cooker, place the washed tongue on it and cover with cold water. Slowly bring to the boil uncovered. Pour off the water and add the vegetables, peppercorns and bouquet garni to the pan, then cover with fresh water. Put on the lid and bring to high (15 lb) pressure. Cook for about 45 minutes (according to

A meal in minutes

weight and thickness of the joint). Reduce pressure slowly.

Remove the tongue from the cooker and allow it to cool slightly before taking off the skin and any gristle and fat. Curl the tongue into a 15-cm (6-in) round cake tin. Put the gelatine in a small bowl and add 30 ml (2 tbsp) cold water, then warm it gently in a pan of hot water until dissolved. Make the gelatine mixture up to 150 ml (¼ pint) with the tongue stock, then pour it over the tongue. Put a plate on top and weigh down with a heavy weight. Leave to set in a cool place. Turn it out and serve sliced.

Lamb boulangère

Cooking time for lamb:
12–14 minutes per 450 g (1 lb)

1·8 kg (4 lb) shoulder of lamb, boned and rolled; boned weight about 1·1 kg (2 ½ lb)
25 g (1 oz) butter
450 g (1 lb) small potatoes, peeled
350 g (12 oz) small onions, skinned
bones from the meat
salt and pepper
2 medium-size cloves of garlic, skinned and crushed
2–3 sprigs of rosemary or 5 ml (1 level tsp) dried rosemary
400 ml (¾ pint) water

Weigh the meat and calculate cooking time, taking into account the thickness of the joint.

Brown the lamb all over in the hot butter in the uncovered pressure cooker. Remove the meat and fry the potatoes and onions until well browned. Remove the vegetables and drain off any fat. Put in the trivet and put the meat and bones on the trivet. Season well, add the garlic and rosemary, and pour in the water. Put on the lid and bring to high (15 lb) pressure, then cook for about 30 minutes (according to weight and thickness of the joint).

Five minutes before the end of the calculated cooking time, reduce pressure quickly and add the vegetables to the cooker. Bring to high (15 lb) pressure, then cook for a further 5 minutes. Reduce pressure quickly. Put the meat on a serving dish with the vegetables surrounding it. Remove bones and rosemary from the cooking liquid and

adjust the seasoning, serve the gravy separately. The gravy may be thickened with 15 ml (1 level tbsp) flour blended with a little of the stock.

Braised stuffed lamb

Cooking time for lamb:
11–12 minutes per 450 g (1 lb)

1·2 kg (2¾ lb) fillet end of leg of lamb, boned weight about 1 kg (2¼ lb)
15 ml (1 tbsp) oil
2 medium-size onions, skinned and sliced
2 carrots, pared and sliced
1 stick of celery, washed and sliced
1 small turnip, peeled and sliced
400 ml (¾ pint) water
bouquet garni
1 clove of garlic, skinned and crushed
15 ml (1 level tbsp) flour

For the stuffing

1 medium-size onion, skinned and finely chopped
25 g (1 oz) butter or margarine
100 g (4 oz) fresh white breadcrumbs
25 g (1 oz) chopped walnuts
25 g (1 oz) sultanas
30 ml (2 tbsp) chopped parsley
salt and pepper
1 egg

Remove the bone from the meat and put it aside. To make the stuffing, lightly fry the onion in the melted fat, then add it to the breadcrumbs and other dry stuffing ingredients. Bind the mixture with the beaten egg and stuff it into the cavity in the meat. Tie or sew the meat with fine string into a neat joint.

Weigh the meat and calculate cooking time, taking into account the thickness of the joint. Brown the joint all over in the heated oil in the uncovered pressure cooker. Remove the joint and fry the vegetables until well browned. Drain off the excess fat, pour in the water and add the seasoning, bouquet garni and garlic. Stand the meat and bones on the vegetables. Put on the lid and bring to high (15 lb) pressure. Cook for about 30 minutes (according to the weight and thickness of the joint). Reduce pressure quickly. Put the meat and vegetables on a hot dish. Discard the bones and bouquet garni. Return the cooker to the heat and bring the cooking liquid to the boil uncovered.

◀ *Spiced vegetables (see page 38)*

Braised stuffed lamb

Blend the flour with a little cold water, and stir in a little of the hot liquid. Return mixture to the pan and bring gravy to the boil, stirring until it thickens. Adjust the seasoning and serve the gravy separately. Redcurrant jelly may also be served as an accompaniment.

Pot au feu

Cooking time for beef:
13–15 minutes per 450 g (1 lb)

This is a meal in itself. Serve the broth with crusty bread, then serve the sliced meat as a main course with the vegetables on a separate dish.

1 kg (2¼ lb) lean beef joint – brisket, topside, leg of mutton cut, silverside
1 large onion, skinned and quartered
1 large carrot, pared and quartered
1 small swede or turnip, peeled and quartered
1 small parsnip, peeled and quartered
2 leeks, quartered and washed
2 sticks of celery, washed and quartered
1·4 litres (2½ pints) water
bouquet garni
10 ml (2 level tsp) salt
pepper
100 g (4 oz) cabbage, washed and quartered

Weigh the meat and calculate cooking time, taking into account the thickness of the joint.

Wipe the meat and put it in the pressure cooker with the prepared vegetables (except the cabbage), water, bouquet garni, salt and pepper. Put on the lid and bring to high (15 lb) pressure, then cook for about 35 minutes (according to weight and thickness of the joint). Reduce pressure quickly. Remove the meat, which should be quite tender, and the bouquet garni.

Put the cabbage in the pressure cooker, put on the lid, bring to high (15 lb) pressure, then cook for 3 minutes. Meanwhile slice the meat thickly. Reduce pressure slowly. Serve the broth, then serve the sliced meat and vegetables separately.

Pot roasted pork with prunes

Cooking time for pork:
12–15 minutes per 450 g (1 lb)

1·4 kg (3 lb) bladebone of pork, boned weight about 1 kg (2¼ lb)
100 g (4 oz) prunes
6–8 sage leaves
salt and pepper
30 ml (2 tbsp) oil
4 onions, skinned and quartered
400 ml (¾ pint) stock or water
2 large cooking apples, peeled and quartered
15 ml (1 level tbsp) brown sugar
15 ml (1 level tbsp) flour

Weigh the meat and calculate cooking time, taking into account the thickness of the joint.

Pour boiling water over the prunes and soak for at least 10 minutes. Lay out the joint, skin side down, on a board and push the sage leaves into the flesh. Sprinkle with salt and pepper, roll up and tie into a neat joint. Fry the meat in the hot oil in the uncovered pressure cooker, until it is well browned all over, especially the skin. Remove the meat and lightly fry the onions. Drain off any remaining oil into a small pan. Put the trivet in the cooker and stand the meat on it, with the onions and strained prunes. Pour on the stock. Put on the lid and bring to high (15 lb) pressure; cook for about 30 minutes (according to thickness and weight of joint).

Four minutes before the end of the calculated cooking time, reduce pressure quickly and strain 300 ml (½ pint) stock into a basin. Put the apples, sprinkled with sugar, in the cooker and put on the lid. Bring to high (15 lb) pressure, then cook for a further 4 minutes. Reduce pressure quickly. Remove the meat and crisp the crackling under a hot grill. Put the meat on a serving dish with the apples and prunes. Meanwhile add the flour to the small pan containing the oil and brown to a good dark colour. Stir the strained stock into the roux and bring to the boil, stirring until the gravy thickens. Adjust seasoning and serve the sauce separately.

Chicken galantine

Cooking time for chicken:
about 15 minutes per 450 g (1 lb)

2·3 kg (5 lb) oven ready chicken, boned weight
   1·3 kg (2¾ lb); chicken bones and giblets
salt and pepper
350 g (12 oz) pork sausage meat
100 g (4 oz) cooked tongue, cut in 1-cm (½-in) dice
100 g (4 oz) cooked ham, cut in 1-cm (½-in) dice
1 onion, skinned and quartered
bouquet garni
1·1 litres (2 pints) water
5 ml (1 level tsp) aspic jelly crystals or gelatine
few cooked vegetables for garnish

The butcher may bone the chicken for you. If not, split the bird down the centre back, and gradually bone out the chicken from either side of the centre back. Reserve the bones to use for the stock.

Spread the bird, skin side down on a board and sprinkle the flesh with salt and pepper. Spread the sausage meat evenly over the surface and then put on the diced tongue and ham. Bring the two sides to overlap and stitch together, using a trussing needle and thin string. Stitch the two ends so that a neat parcel is formed. Weigh the chicken and calculate cooking time. Put the chicken in the centre of a piece of foil and fold tightly into shape.

Put the chicken bones, giblets, onion, bouquet garni and seasoning in the pressure cooker. Pour on the water and put in the chicken. Put on the lid and bring to high (15 lb) pressure. Cook for about 40 minutes (according to weight). Reduce pressure quickly. Remove the chicken and stand it on a dish. Cover it with another dish, put a weight on it and leave until cold.

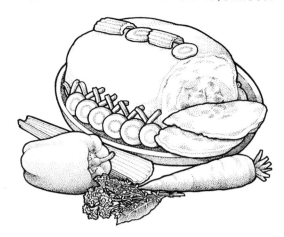

Chicken galantine

Meanwhile strain the stock and leave it to cool so that fat settles on top. Scrape off the fat and measure 150 ml (¼ pint) stock. Sprinkle the aspic crystals or gelatine over 15 ml (1 tbsp) cold stock in a bowl, leave for a few minutes. Then stand the bowl in a pan of hot water to dissolve the gelatine or aspic. Stir it into the rest of the stock and leave until it is almost setting and has a syrupy consistency. Remove foil and string from the chicken and pour over the jelly, decorate with cooked vegetables and leave to set. Trim and serve sliced with salad.

Country style terrine of liver

100 g (4 oz) stewing veal, minced
100 g (4 oz) streaky pork, minced
225 g (8 oz) pig's liver, minced
100 g (4 oz) chicken livers, minced
1 clove of garlic, skinned and crushed
2·5 ml (½ level tsp) salt
1·25 ml (¼ level tsp) freshly ground pepper
1·25 ml (¼ level tsp) ground allspice
4–6 thin rashers of streaky bacon, rinded
2 bayleaves
10 ml (2 tsp) brandy

Put all the meats, garlic and spices together in a bowl and mix well. Put the mixture in a 15-cm (6-in) soufflé dish or ovenproof terrine and press down well. Arrange the bacon rashers over the top and put on the bay leaves. Cover lightly with a piece of foil. Put 600 ml (1 pint) water in the pressure cooker, put in the trivet and stand the terrine on it. Put on the lid and bring to high (15 lb) pressure. Cook for about 40 minutes. (Cooking time depends on the thickness of the dish. To test, reduce pressure quickly, remove dish from the cooker and pierce with a skewer. If there are signs of blood, cook a little longer.) Reduce pressure quickly. Remove dish from cooker. Make a few holes in the terrine with a skewer and pour over the brandy. Make a round of foil the size of the dish and put this over the terrine, put weights on top and leave to cool. When cold, remove excess fat and bayleaves. Serve sliced with toast or salad.

Chicken pot roast with walnuts

See colour picture on cover

**Cooking time for chicken:
6–8 minutes per 450 g (1 lb)**

1 oven ready chicken about 1·6 kg (3 ½ lb)
25 g (1 oz) butter
15 ml (1 tbsp) oil
350 g (12 oz) celery, washed and sliced
225 g (8 oz) carrots, pared and cut into chunks
225 g (8 oz) leeks, trimmed, sliced and washed
50 g (2 oz) button mushrooms
25 g (1 oz) walnuts
300 ml (½ pint) chicken stock
salt and pepper
30 ml (2 level tbsp) cornflour

For the stuffing
knob of butter
½ small onion, skinned and finely chopped
25 g (1 oz) mushrooms, finely chopped
30 ml (2 level tbsp) chopped walnuts
25 g (1 oz) fresh white breadcrumbs
5 ml (1 tsp) freshly chopped parsley
1 small egg, beaten
salt and freshly ground pepper

First make the stuffing. Melt the butter in the pressure cooker, add the onion and mushrooms and sauté uncovered until the onion is soft, about 5 minutes. Turn mixture into a bowl, add the walnuts, breadcrumbs and parsley with sufficient egg to bind. Season to taste. Stuff the neck cavity

of the chicken and truss. Weigh the chicken and calculate cooking time.

Melt the butter and oil in uncovered pressure cooker and fry the chicken until brown all over. Remove chicken from the cooker. Add the vegetables and sauté uncovered for 5 minutes. Return the chicken to the pressure cooker with the walnuts, stock and seasoning. Put on the lid and bring up to high (15 lb) pressure, then cook for about 25 minutes (according to weight). Reduce pressure quickly. Lift out the chicken and place it on a serving dish. Blend the cornflour with a little water to a smooth paste. Add it to the juices in the cooker, stirring. Bring back to the boil, stirring, and cook until gravy thickens. Serve vegetables and gravy separately.

Galantine of veal

**Cooking time for veal:
20 minutes per 450 g (1 lb)**

900 g (2 lb) breast of veal, boned weight about 675 g (1 ½ lb); cut in one thin piece
1 large onion, skinned and quartered
1 large carrot, pared and sliced
bouquet garni
600 ml (1 pint) water
salt and pepper

For the stuffing
1 medium-size onion, skinned and chopped
25 g (1 oz) butter
100 g (4 oz) pork, minced
150 g (6 oz) ham or cold bacon, minced
50 g (2 oz) fresh breadcrumbs
2·5 ml (½ level tsp) dried thyme
5 ml (1 level tsp) grated lemon rind
salt and pepper
1 small egg

First make the stuffing. Lightly fry the onion in melted butter until just tender. Stir in the pork, ham and breadcrumbs. Add the thyme and lemon rind. Season well and bind with the egg.

Spread the boned breast of veal on a board and put on the stuffing; roll up the veal and sew it into a sausage shape. Weigh the meat and calculate cooking time. Wrap meat in a piece of greased foil and fold tightly into shape, making sure the ends are sealed. Put the trivet in the pressure cooker, put the veal parcel and any bones on the trivet and add vegetables, bouquet garni, water and seasoning. Put on the lid and bring to high (15 lb) pressure. Cook for about 45 minutes (according to weight of the joint). Reduce pressure quickly. Remove the galantine. Tighten the foil and press the galantine between two plates with a weight on top and leave until cold. Strain off the stock and use it to glaze the galantine when cold. Test a little stock to make sure it jells before glazing.

Pork brawn

Ask your butcher to remove the brains and tongue of the head for use separately.

½ **pickled pig's head**
bouquet garni
6 peppercorns
1 large onion, skinned and quartered
1 small carrot, pared
1 hardboiled egg

Wash the head thoroughly making sure the ear and nostril are well scrubbed. Soak in fresh water for about 1 hour. Cut off the ear and scald it, then scrape off any hair and wash well again. Tie the brains and tongue in a piece of muslin. Put the head with the ear, muslin bag, bouquet garni, peppercorns and vegetables into the cooker. Cover with water (the cooker must not be more than half full). Bring to high (15 lb) pressure, then cook for 40 minutes. Reduce pressure slowly.

Remove the muslin bag and chop the brain, skin the tongue and cut into 2·5-cm (1-in) pieces. Remove the flesh from the bones. Slice the egg and arrange it in a mould. Put all the meat in the mould, strain the stock, adjust the seasoning and pour stock into the mould to fill. Leave to get cold and firmly set. Scrape the fat from the top of the brawn before turning it out. Serve with salad.

Meat loaf

350 g (12 oz) minced beef
100 g (4 oz) sausagemeat
1 onion, skinned and finely chopped
5 ml (1 level tsp) mixed herbs
15 ml (1 level tbsp) tomato ketchup
15 ml (1 level tbsp) HP sauce
salt and pepper
25 g (1 oz) white breadcrumbs
1 egg, beaten

In a mixing bowl, stir the minced beef and sausagemeat together until well blended. Add the remaining ingredients and mix well. Shape the mixture into a thick roll that will fit into the pressure cooker. Wrap it in foil, pleating it to allow for expansion. Seal each end tightly. Put the trivet in the pressure cooker, place the foil-wrapped loaf on top and add 600 ml (1 pint) hot water. Put the lid on the cooker, bring up to high (15 lb) pressure, then cook for 25 minutes. Reduce pressure quickly. Serve hot with tomato sauce or cold with salads.

Guide to pressure cooking meat and poultry

In all cases allow 300 ml (½ pint) liquid for up to 900 g (2 lb) meat for the first 15 minutes cooking time, then add 150 ml (¼ pint) for every 450 g (1 lb). Cooking times will vary according to the thickness and quality of the meat, so the times here are only approximate. When stuffing boned and rolled joints, take into account the type and quantity of stuffing used. Weigh the meat and calculate the cooking time after the final preparation. All the joints and cuts given below are suitable for pot roasts and braised dishes except those marked 'boiling only'.

Meat	Joints and cuts	Pressure cooking time at (15 lb) pressure
Beef		
joints without bone	buttock steak in pieces	8 minutes
	topside	12–15 minutes per 450 g (1 lb)
	top rump	12–15 minutes per 450 g (1 lb)
boned and rolled	middle rib	10–12 minutes per 450 g (1 lb)
	leg of mutton cut	10–12 minutes per 450 g (1 lb)
	silverside	13–15 minutes per 450 g (1 lb)
	brisket	13–15 minutes per 450 g (1 lb)
	flank	13–15 minutes per 450 g (1 lb)
pickled joints	brisket (boiling only)	13–15 minutes per 450 g (1 lb)
	silverside (boiling only)	13–15 minutes per 450 g (1 lb)
	flank (boiling only)	13–15 minutes per 450 g (1 lb)
	tongue (boiling only)	15 minutes per 450 g (1 lb)
Offal	oxtail (jointed)	40 minutes
	tongue (fresh)	15 minutes per 450 g (1 lb)
	sweetbreads	6 minutes
	lambs hearts (whole)	20 minutes
	ox heart (sliced)	20 minutes
	kidneys	5 minutes
	brains	5 minutes
Lamb		
on the bone	best end of neck	10–12 minutes per 450 g (1 lb)
	loin	10–12 minutes per 450 g (1 lb)
	shoulder	10–12 minutes per 450 g (1 lb)
	leg-fillet or knuckle end	10–12 minutes per 450 g (1 lb)
	cutlets and chops	6 minutes
boned and rolled	best end of neck	11–12 minutes per 450 (1 lb)
	loin	11–12 minutes per 450 g (1 lb)
	shoulder	12–14 minutes per 450 g (1 lb)
	leg	11–12 minutes per 450 g (1 lb)

Meat	Joints and cuts	Pressure cooking time at (15 lb) pressure
Veal		
on the bone	knuckle	12 minutes per 450 g (1 lb)
	cutlets and chops	10 minutes
boned and rolled	leg-fillet	10 minutes per 450 g (1 lb)
	shoulder	11–12 minutes per 450 g (1 lb)
	loin	11–12 minutes per 450 g (1 lb)
	breast	10–12 minutes per 450 g (1 lb)
	neck (boiling only)	11–12 minutes per 450 g (1 lb)
Pork and bacon		
on the bone	chops	6–10 minutes
	blade bone	11–12 minutes per 450 g (1 lb)
	trotters (boiling only)	20 minutes
	head (boiling only)	20 minutes
boned and rolled	blade bone	12–15 minutes per 450 g (1 lb)
	hand and spring	12–15 minutes per 450 g (1 lb)
	belly	12–15 minutes per 450 g (1 lb)
pickled	bacon joints	10–14 minutes per 450 g (1 lb)
	belly (boiling only)	12–15 minutes per 450 g (1 lb)
	trotters (boiling only)	25 minutes
	head (boiling only)	25 minutes
Poultry and game		
chicken	spring and poussin	4–6 minutes per 450 g (1 lb)
	roasting 1·1 kg (2½ lb)	6–8 minutes per 450 g (1 lb)
	1·3 kg (3½ lb)	6–8 minutes per 450 g (1 lb)
	boiling fowl 2·2 kg (5 lb)	10–12 minutes per 450 g (1 lb)
	3·1 kg (7 lb) halved	10–12 minutes per 450 g (1 lb)
	joints or pieces	4–6 minutes
turkey	joints or pieces	10–15 minutes
duckling	whole 1·3 kg (3½ lb)	6–8 minutes per 450 g (1 lb)
	halved 2–2·7 kg (4¼–6 lb)	4–5 minutes per 450 g (1 lb)
pheasant	whole young 700 g (1½ lb)	6–8 minutes per 450 g (1 lb)
	whole old 1 kg (2 lb 2 oz)	10–12 minutes per 450 g (1 lb)
	halved or jointed	4–5 minutes per 450 g (1 lb)
pigeon	whole young 450 g (1 lb)	15 minutes
	whole old 450 g (1 lb)	20 minutes
	halved	12 minutes
hare	jointed	30 minutes
rabbit	jointed	12–15 minutes

STEWS, CASSEROLES AND MEAT PUDDINGS

When stews and casseroles are made in a pressure cooker the cooking time is reduced to about a quarter, or less, of the normal cooking time. As the meat or poultry is usually cut into small pieces or portions they tenderise very quickly under pressure. With the reduction in cooking time, and very little evaporation, less liquid is required for most recipes. When using a recipe which requires chicken joints, remember it is cheaper to buy a whole chicken and joint it than to buy separate joints.

Adapting recipes for the pressure cooker

Most stew and casserole recipes can be adapted to use in the pressure cooker. The amount of liquid should be reduced by a quarter, leaving approximately three quarters of the normal amount required, but never use less than 300 ml (½ pint). The cooking time can be reduced to between 15 minutes to 30 minutes depending upon the quality, cut and size of the meat. It should be remembered that stews and casseroles should not be thickened until the end of the cooking time, otherwise the thickening agent will stick and burn on the base of the cooker. The thickening agent is usually added as a roux, beurre manié or blended to a cream with a little cold liquid. In all cases the thickening must be thoroughly cooked in the open pressure cooker; stir or whisk whilst bringing to the boil.

Adding vegetables

In some recipes, all the vegetables are cooked with the meat to impart their flavour to the gravy. In other recipes some of the vegetables are added towards the end of the cooking. This is done by reducing the pressure of the cooker, adding the vegetables and then bringing the cooker to pressure again for the rest of the cooking time. Likewise, extra vegetables to complete the meal may be added, in containers, a few minutes towards the end of the cooking time. When estimating cooking time for vegetables, take into account their age and freshness, allowing a little longer when more mature.

Cooking large quantities

A pressure cooker is particularly useful for making bulk quantities of stews or casseroles for the freezer (see page 112). Whatever the quantity made, it still requires the same cooking time. But it should be remembered that the cooker must never be more than three quarters full.

Making meat puddings in the pressure cooker

Meat puddings with a suet crust may also be cooked successfully in a pressure cooker. It is best to cook the filling before making the pudding, which can then be cooked in approximately a fifth of the normal time (see page 58 steak and kidney pudding).

Burgundy beef

450 g (1 lb) topside
25 g (1 oz) butter or margarine
100 g (4 oz) piece of streaky bacon, rinded and diced
8 small onions or shallots, skinned
100 g (4 oz) button mushrooms
15 ml (1 level tbsp) flour
45 ml (3 tbsp) brandy (optional)
150 ml (¼ pint) burgundy or other red wine
150 ml (¼ pint) stock
pinch of thyme
bayleaf
1 clove of garlic, skinned and crushed
salt and pepper

Cut the meat into 4-cm (1½-in) cubes and brown in the fat in the uncovered pressure cooker. Remove the meat from the cooker and fry the bacon until it is well browned, then put it with the meat. Drain off the excess fat, leaving just over 15 ml (1 tbsp) in the cooker and fry the shallots until well browned, then fry the button mushrooms. Put the shallots and mushrooms aside for the garnish. Stir the flour into remaining fat and cook until well browned, then remove this roux from the cooker to use later for thickening.

Pour the brandy into the cooker and set it alight. While the brandy is flaming, return the meats to the cooker with the wine, stock, thyme, bayleaf and garlic; add seasoning. Put on the lid and bring to high (15 lb) pressure. Cook for 15 minutes. Reduce pressure quickly. Add the shallots and mushrooms to the cooker. Bring to high (15 lb) pressure and cook for a further 5 minutes. Reduce pressure quickly. Put the meat and garnish on a hot dish. Remove the bayleaf. Stir in the browned roux and reboil the gravy, whisking while it thickens. Adjust seasoning and pour the gravy over the meat. Serve with creamed potatoes.

Beef olives

Beef olives

8 thin slices of topside of beef
30 ml (2 tbsp) oil
3 onions, skinned and sliced
15 ml (1 level tbsp) flour
400 ml (¾ pint) stock
bouquet garni
salt and pepper

For the stuffing
50 g (2 oz) shredded suet
50 g (2 oz) ham or boiled bacon, finely chopped
100 g (4 oz) fresh breadcrumbs
15 ml (1 tbsp) chopped parsley
1·25 ml (¼ level tsp) dried mixed herbs
salt and pepper
1 egg, beaten

Mix the dry ingredients for the stuffing and bind with the beaten egg. Spread the slices of beef with the stuffing, roll them up and tie with cotton or fine string. Heat the oil in the uncovered pressure cooker and fry the beef olives until they are well browned. Remove the meat from the cooker and fry the onions until lightly browned. Put the onions with the meat, sprinkle flour into the cooker and cook until it is well browned. Remove this roux and keep aside to use later. Put the beef olives, onions, stock, bouquet garni and seasoning in the cooker. Cover with lid and bring to high (15 lb) pressure. Cook for 20 minutes. Reduce pressure quickly.

Remove beef olives from the cooker. Discard the bayleaf. Stir in the browned roux and bring the gravy to the boil, stirring until it thickens. Cut the string from the olives, pile them in a hot dish and pour over the gravy. Serve with creamed potatoes.

Carbonade of beef

700 g (1 ½ lb) stewing steak
45 ml (3 tbsp) oil
4 lean bacon rashers, rinded and chopped
300 ml (½ pint) brown ale
150 ml (¼ pint) stock
30 ml (2 tbsp) vinegar
3 large onions, skinned and sliced
1 clove of garlic, skinned and crushed
bouquet garni
salt
freshly ground pepper
15 ml (1 level tbsp) cornflour

Cut the meat into 2·5-cm (1-in) cubes. Heat the oil in the uncovered pressure cooker and quickly fry the meat until it is brown on all sides. Add the bacon and continue cooking for 1 minute. Stir in the beer, stock and vinegar. Add onions, garlic, bouquet garni and seasoning. Put on lid, bring up to high (15 lb) pressure. Cook for 20 minutes. Reduce pressure quickly. Remove the bouquet garni. Blend the cornflour to a smooth cream with

a little water, then stir in a little of the hot cooking liquid. Add the mixture to the cooker, bring back to the boil, stirring, and cook until the gravy thickens. Serve with boiled potatoes or rice.
SERVES 4–6

Australian beef hotpot

700 g (1 ½ lb) chuck steak
30 ml (2 tbsp) oil
1 large onion, skinned and sliced
1 small cooking apple, peeled, cored and diced
15 ml (1 level tbsp) curry powder
226-g (8-oz) can of tomatoes
50 g (2 oz) seedless raisins
300 ml (½ pint) beef stock
salt
freshly ground pepper
15 ml (1 level tbsp) brown sugar
15 ml (1 level tbsp) cornflour

Slice the meat thinly and cut it into 2·5-cm (1-in) squares. Heat the oil in the uncovered pressure cooker and brown the meat on all sides. Remove the meat from the cooker. Put the onion and apple in the cooker and cook until the onion is soft, for about 3 minutes. Add the curry powder and cook for 1 more minute, stirring. Then stir in the tomatoes with juice, raisins, stock, seasoning and brown sugar and bring to the boil uncovered. Return the meat to the cooker. Put on the lid and bring to high (15 lb) pressure. Cook for 15 minutes. Reduce pressure quickly. Blend the cornflour to a smooth cream with a little water and stir in a little of the hot cooking liquid. Add the mixture to the cooker and bring back to the boil, stirring, and cook until the gravy thickens.
SERVES 4–5

Beef and pepper casserole

See colour picture facing page 64.

700 g (1 ½ lb) stewing steak
30 ml (2 level tbsp) flour
salt and pepper
30 ml (2 tbsp) oil
2 large onions, skinned and sliced
2 green peppers, seeded and finely sliced
300 ml (½ pint) beef stock
15 ml (1 level tbsp) tomato paste

Cut the meat into 4-cm (1 ½-in) cubes and toss it in seasoned flour. Heat the oil in the uncovered pressure cooker, add the onion and green pepper and cook until the onion is soft, for about 3 minutes. Remove the vegetables from the cooker. Add the meat to pressure cooker, a few pieces at a time, and brown it on all sides. Remove the cooker from heat and stir in the stock and tomato paste. Return the onion and pepper to the cooker. Put on the lid and bring to high (15 lb) pressure. Cook for 20 minutes. Reduce pressure quickly. Serve with a green salad and crusty French bread.
SERVES 4–5

Steak and kidney pudding

450 g (1 lb) stewing steak
100 g (4 oz) lamb's or ox kidney
15 ml (1 level tbsp) seasoned flour
1 onion, skinned and chopped
300 ml (½ pint) stock or water

For the suet crust pastry
225 g (8 oz) self raising flour
2·5 ml (½ level tsp) salt
100 g (4 oz) shredded suet
about 150 ml (¼ pint) cold water

Cut the meat into 2-cm (¾-in) dice. Remove the skin and core from kidneys and cut the kidney into small pieces. Toss the steak and kidney in the seasoned flour. Put the meat in the pressure cooker with the onion and stock. Put on the lid and bring to high (15 lb) pressure. Cook for 15 minutes. Reduce the pressure quickly. Leave the meat to cool.

Grease a 900-ml (1 ½-pint) pudding basin. Make the pastry by mixing the dry ingredients to a soft dough with the cold water. Knead the dough lightly on a floured board and cut off a quarter for the lid. Roll the pastry into a large round and line the basin with it. Damp the top edge. Roll out the remaining pastry to form a lid. Spoon the meat filling into the prepared basin, adding only half the cooking liquid. Put on the pastry lid and seal the edges together. Cover with a piece of greased foil and tie a piece of string round the rim, then over the top to form a handle. Put 1 litre (2 pints) water in the pressure cooker, put in the trivet and bring the water to the boil. Lower the pudding into the cooker, put on the lid without the weight and lower the heat so that the cooker steams gently for 15 minutes. There should be a steady but gentle flow of steam escaping from the cooker. At the end of the pre-steaming time, increase the heat and bring the cooker to low (5 lb) pressure. Then continue to cook for 30 minutes. Reduce pressure slowly. Remove the pudding and, before serving, cut a wedge from the top crust and fill the pudding with the remaining gravy, reheated.

Bacon roly-poly

350 g (12 oz) streaky bacon or bacon bits, rinded and diced
2 medium-size onions, skinned and chopped
30 ml (2 tbsp) chopped parsley
freshly ground pepper

For the suet crust pastry
225 g (8 oz) self raising flour
2·5 ml (1 level tsp) salt
100 g (4 oz) shredded suet
about 150 ml (¼ pint) cold water

Gently fry the diced bacon in a frying pan, so that the fat runs out and the bacon browns. Put it in a basin while lightly frying the onion in the bacon fat. Cook the onion until it is just tender. Mix it with the bacon, parsley and pepper.

To make the suet crust pastry, mix the dry ingredients to a soft dough with the water. Knead the dough, on a floured surface and roll it into a rectangle about 18 × 23 cm (7 × 9 in). Damp the edges with water. Sprinkle on the filling and roll up the dough from a narrow end. Make a pleat in a large piece of greased foil and place the roly-poly on it. Fold the foil tightly to encase the pudding, making sure the edges are well sealed. Put 1 litre (1¾ pints) water in the pressure cooker, put in trivet and bring to the boil. Gently lower pudding on to the trivet. Put on the lid without the weight and lower the heat so that a steady but gentle stream of steam escapes through the open vent. Let the cooker steam for 10 minutes, then put on the weight and increase the heat to bring to low (5 lb) pressure. Cook for 30 minutes. Reduce pressure slowly. Turn out the pudding and serve with gravy or tomato sauce (see page 81).

Lamb hotch potch

See colour picture facing page 65

1 kg (2¼ lb) middle neck of lamb
salt and pepper
45 ml (3 tbsp) oil
3 medium-size onions, skinned and sliced
2 sticks of celery, washed, trimmed and sliced
2 leeks, washed and sliced
3 medium-size carrots, scraped
1 small swede, peeled
600 ml (1 pint) stock
50 g (2 oz) pearl barley
4–6 cooked potatoes
15 ml (1 tbsp) chopped parsley

Have the lamb cut into manageable pieces and trim off excess fat and gristle. Season the meat. Heat 30 ml (2 tbsp) oil in the uncovered pressure cooker and fry the meat until it is brown on both sides. Remove the meat and fry the onions, celery and leeks for about 3 minutes. Cut the carrots and swede into 5-cm (2-in) sticks. Drain off any fat from the cooker and stir in the carrots, swedes, meat, stock, pearl barley and a little more seasoning. Put on the lid and bring to high (15 lb) pressure. Cook for 20 minutes.

Meanwhile, cut the potatoes into rough pieces and fry them in the remaining oil in a frying pan until they are well browned. Reduce cooker pressure quickly. Serve the hotch potch with the potatoes arranged round the edge and sprinkle with parsley.

Hotpot

8 small lamb cutlets
15 ml (1 tbsp) oil
2 lamb's kidneys, skinned, cored and halved
225 g (8 oz) onions, skinned and sliced
450 g (1 lb) potatoes, peeled and sliced
15 ml (1 tbsp) chopped parsley
salt and pepper
300 ml (½ pint) stock
10 ml (2 level tsp) tomato paste
25 g (1 oz) dripping or butter

Trim excess fat from the cutlets and lightly fry them in the oil in open cooker until they are brown on both sides. Remove the meat and lightly fry the kidneys. Remove kidneys from cooker. Take a

1·1-litre (2-pint) casserole or ovenproof dish and arrange the meat, vegetables and parsley in it in layers, seasoning between layers and finishing with a thick layer of potatoes.

Add 15–30 ml (1–2 tbsp) of the stock to the drippings in the pan, heat gently and scrape well. Then add the pan juices, the tomato paste and the stock to the contents of the casserole. Cover with foil. Put 600 ml (1 pint) water in the pressure cooker, put in the trivet and stand the casserole on it. Cover with the lid and bring to high (15 lb) pressure. Cook for 35 minutes. Reduce pressure quickly. Remove the casserole from pan, dot the potatoes with dripping and put under a hot grill to brown. If the casserole dish tends to craze protect the edges with foil before grilling.

Summer lamb casserole

Cooking time for lamb:
10–12 minutes per 450 g (1 lb)

900 g (2 lb) neck of lamb
25 g (1 oz) dripping or lard
300 ml (½ pint) beef stock
15 ml (1 level tbsp) tomato paste
salt
freshly ground pepper
450 g (1 lb) new carrots, scraped
450 g (1 lb) new potatoes, scraped
225 g (½ lb) frozen peas, or fresh shelled peas
15 ml (1 level tbsp) cornflour
freshly chopped mint, optional

Weigh the lamb and calculate cooking time, taking into account the thickness of the joint.

Melt the fat in the uncovered pressure cooker and lightly fry the meat on all sides; drain off the surplus fat. Add the stock, tomato paste and seasoning; bring to the boil, stirring. Put the lid on the cooker and bring to high (15 lb) pressure. Cook for about 20 minutes.

Five minutes before the end of the calculated cooking time, reduce pressure quickly and add the carrots and potatoes. Replace the lid and bring back to high (15 lb) pressure. Cook for a further 5 minutes. Reduce pressure quickly. Remove the meat from the cooker, add the peas and continue cooking with the cooker loosely covered. Meanwhile, remove bones from the lamb, cut the meat

into even-sized chunks and return it to the cooker to reheat. Blend the cornflour to a smooth paste with a little water, stir in a little of the hot cooking liquid and add the mixture to the cooker. Bring the gravy to the boil, stirring, until it thickens and cook until the peas are tender. Serve sprinkled with mint.

Lamb Avignon

The meat in this recipe is marinaded for about 6 hours, so start the preparations several hours ahead of the meal.

1 leg of lamb about 1·8 kg (4 lb)
30 ml (2 tbsp) chopped parsley
2 cloves of garlic, skinned and crushed
salt and pepper
3 onions, skinned and sliced
3 carrots, pared and sliced
300 ml (½ pint) red wine
100 g (4 oz) green bacon, rinded and diced
30 ml (2 tbsp) oil
30 ml (2 tbsp) brandy
thinly pared rind of ½ small orange
bouquet garni
300 ml (½ pint) water
8–10 black olives
30 ml (2 level tbsp) flour, optional

Cut the meat from the bone and divide it into 5–cm (2-in) pieces. Put the meat in a dish with the chopped parsley, garlic and seasoning. Sprinkle half the sliced vegetables over the meat and pour on the wine. Leave to marinade for about 6 hours, stirring now and again.

Strain the marinade ingredients from the meat and reserve the liquid. Lightly fry the bacon in the heated oil in the uncovered pressure cooker, then remove the bacon and fry the meat and vegetables until they are well browned. Pour on the brandy and set it alight, then add the marinading liquid, orange rind and bouquet garni. Pour on the water and put on the lid. Bring to high (15 lb) pressure. Cook for 15 minutes. Reduce pressure quickly. Remove the bouquet garni. If wished, the gravy may be thickened. To do this, mix the flour to a smooth cream with a little cold water. Stir in a little of the hot gravy, then add the mixture to the cooker. Bring the gravy to the boil, uncovered, stirring until it thickens. Add the black olives and serve.

Haricot beans make an excellent accompaniment to this dish.

Lamb chops with peppers

4 loin lamb chops
salt
freshly ground pepper
25 g (1 oz) butter or margarine
1 large onion, skinned and thinly sliced
3 streaky bacon rashers, rinded and chopped
1 clove of garlic, skinned and crushed
thinly pared rind of 1 lemon, cut into thin strips
30 ml (2 tbsp) lemon juice
30 ml (2 level tbsp) caster sugar
1 red pepper, seeded and thinly sliced
10 ml (2 level tsp) paprika pepper
425-g (15-oz) can of tomatoes, use juice

Trim the chops and season well. Melt the fat in the uncovered pressure cooker and quickly brown the chops on both sides. Remove the chops from the cooker, then add the onion and bacon and cook until the onion is soft, for about 3 minutes. Add the remaining ingredients and stir well. Return the chops to the cooker. Put on lid and bring to high (15 lb) pressure. Cook for 6 minutes. Reduce pressure quickly. Serve the chops with the sauce spooned over them.

Haricot lamb

100 g (4 oz) haricot beans
1·1 kg (2½ lb) middle neck of lamb
15 ml (1 tbsp) oil
2 onions, skinned and sliced
2 medium carrots, pared and diced
1 medium turnip, peeled and diced
600 ml (1 pint) stock
salt and pepper
bouquet garni
30 ml (2 level tbsp) flour
15 ml (1 tbsp) chopped parsley

Wash the beans, pour boiling water over them and leave to soak for at least 1 hour. Cut the lamb into neat pieces and fry it in the hot oil in the uncovered pressure cooker until well browned. Remove the

meat and fry the onion. Drain off excess fat and return the meat to the cooker with the drained beans, a few pieces of the carrot and turnip, stock, seasoning and bouquet garni. Put on the lid and bring to high (15 lb) pressure. Cook for 15 minutes. Reduce pressure slowly. Add remaining vegetables, put on the lid and bring to high (15 lb) pressure again, then cook for 5 more minutes. Reduce pressure slowly.

Place the meat and vegetables on a hot serving dish. Discard the bouquet garni. Blend the flour to a smooth paste with a little cold water and stir in a little of the hot cooking liquid. Add the mixture to the cooker and bring to the boil uncovered, stirring as it thickens. Pour the gravy over the meat and vegetables and serve garnished with parsley.

Midweek bacon stew

100 g (4 oz) butter beans
700 g (1½ lb) bacon slipper joint
225 g (8 oz) turnip, peeled and sliced
225 g (8 oz) parsnip, peeled and sliced
25 g (1 oz) butter
freshly ground pepper
900 ml (1½ pints) stock
30 ml (2 level tbsp) flour
7·5 ml (1½ level tsp) dry mustard
chopped parsley

Wash the beans, pour boiling water over them and

Midweek bacon stew

leave to soak for at least 1 hour. Remove the rind from the bacon and cut the meat into 2·5-cm (1-in) cubes. Put into the pressure cooker and cover with water. Cover the pressure cooker with the lid (but without the weight) and bring to the boil. Remove cooker from the heat, drain off the liquid and keep the bacon separate. Fry the prepared vegetables in the butter in the uncovered pressure cooker until well browned. Return the bacon, drained beans, freshly ground pepper and stock to the cooker. Put on the lid and bring to high (15 lb) pressure. Cook for 20 minutes. Reduce the pressure slowly. Blend the flour and mustard with a little cold water, then stir in a little of the hot stock. Add the mixture to the cooker and bring to the boil uncovered, stirring until the gravy thickens. Put the contents of the cooker in a hot dish and serve sprinkled with the parsley.

Spring chicken casserole

1 small chicken about 1·1 kg (2 ½ lb)
25 g (1 oz) butter or margarine
2 medium-size onions, skinned and sliced
350 g (12 oz) small carrots, pared
396-g (14-oz) can of tomatoes
600 ml (1 pint) chicken stock
salt and pepper
30 ml (2 level tbsp) flour

For the parsley dumplings
100 g (4 oz) self raising flour
50 g (2 oz) shredded suet
1·25 ml (¼ level tsp) salt
pinch of pepper
15 ml (1 tbsp) chopped parsley
about 75 ml (5 tbsp) cold water

Cut the chicken into eight pieces and remove the skin. Fry the chicken pieces in the fat in the uncovered pressure cooker until they are well browned. Remove the chicken and fry the onions until they are just golden. Return the chicken to the cooker with the carrots, drained tomatoes (reserving the juice), stock and seasoning. Put on the lid and bring to high (15 lb) pressure. Cook for 10 minutes. Meanwhile, make the parsley dumplings by mixing the dry ingredients to a soft dough with the water. Divide the dough into eight balls.

Reduce the cooker pressure quickly. Bring the contents of the cooker to boiling point, uncovered and add the dumplings. Put on the lid and lower the heat to allow the cooker to steam gently but steadily for 3 minutes. Then increase the heat to bring to low (5 lb) pressure and cook a further 4 minutes. Reduce pressure quickly. Put the chicken, vegetables and dumplings in a deep casserole. Blend the flour to a smooth cream with a little of the tomato juice and stir in some of the hot cooking liquid. Add the mixture to the cooker and bring to the boil uncovered, stirring until the sauce thickens. Pour the sauce over the chicken joints.

Chicken Marengo

4 chicken joints
15 ml (1 tbsp) oil
50 g (2 oz) streaky bacon, rinded and chopped
1 large onion, skinned and chopped
1 stick of celery, washed, trimmed and chopped
50 g (2 oz) mushroom stalks, chopped
45 ml (3 level tbsp) flour
25 g (1 oz) butter
1 clove of garlic, skinned and crushed
425-g (15-oz) can of tomatoes
150 ml (¼ pint) chicken stock
salt and pepper
bouquet garni
30 ml (2 tbsp) sherry
100 g (4 oz) button mushrooms

Fry the chicken joints in the heated oil in the uncovered pressure cooker until they are well browned all over. Remove the chicken from cooker and fry the bacon and vegetables. Remove the vegetables and brown the flour, adding a little butter if necessary. When the flour is well browned, remove it from cooker to use later. Return the chicken and vegetables to the cooker with the garlic, tomatoes with juice, stock, seasoning and bouquet garni. Put on the lid and bring to high (15 lb) pressure. Cook for 4–6 minutes. Reduce pressure quickly.

Take out the bouquet garni and put the chicken on a hot dish. Fry the button mushrooms in the rest of the butter in a separate pan. Sieve the rest of the ingredients or purée them in an electric blender. Return the purée to the cooker with the browned flour and sherry. Bring to the boil, uncovered, whisking until the sauce thickens.

Pour the sauce over the chicken and garnish with the button mushrooms.

Chicken with lemon cream sauce

4 chicken joints, skinned
30 ml (2 level tbsp) flour
salt and pepper
50 g (2 oz) butter or margarine
grated rind and juice of 1 lemon
1 medium-size onion, skinned and chopped
90 ml (6 tbsp) dry white wine
300 ml (½ pint) chicken stock
15 ml (1 level tbsp) cornflour
142-ml (¼-pint) carton of single cream

Cut each joint in half and coat in seasoned flour. Melt the fat in the uncovered pressure cooker and brown the chicken evenly. Add the lemon juice, onion, wine and stock. Put on the lid and bring up to high (15 lb) pressure. Cook for 4–6 minutes. Reduce pressure quickly. Remove the chicken joints and put them in a hot dish. Blend the cornflour to a smooth cream with a little cold water, then add a little of the hot cooking liquid. Add the mixture to the cooker with the lemon rind and bring to the boil uncovered, stirring until the sauce thickens. Add the cream and heat through, but do not boil. Adjust seasoning. Pour the sauce over the chicken.

Chicken chasseur

4 chicken joints
15 ml (1 tbsp) oil
25 g (1 oz) butter
1 onion, skinned and chopped
100 g (4 oz) mushrooms, sliced
30 ml (2 level tbsp) flour
2 tomatoes, skinned and diced
15 ml (1 level tbsp) tomato paste
salt and pepper
300 ml (½ pint) stock
60 ml (4 tbsp) white wine
bouquet garni
15 ml (1 tbsp) chopped parsley
15 ml (1 tbsp) chopped chives

Fry the chicken joints in the hot oil and butter in the uncovered pressure cooker until they are well browned. Remove the chicken and brown the onion and mushrooms, then put them with the chicken. Sprinkle the flour in the cooker and cook until it is well browned, then take it out and put aside for later use. Put all other ingredients, except the parsley and chives, in the cooker. Put on the lid and bring to high (15 lb) pressure. Cook for 8 minutes. Put the chicken and vegetables in a hot casserole. Remove the bouquet garni. Stir the browned flour into the cooker and bring to the boil, uncovered, whisking until the sauce thickens. Pour the sauce over the chicken and sprinkle with the herbs.

Chicken paprika

2 medium-size onions, skinned and sliced
2 small green peppers, seeded and sliced
30 ml (2 tbsp) oil
15 ml (1 level tbsp) paprika pepper
1 large clove of garlic, skinned and crushed
4 tomatoes, skinned and chopped
300 ml (½ pint) chicken stock
salt and pepper
4 chicken joints
15 ml (1 level tbsp) cornflour
141-g (5-fl oz) carton of yoghurt

Lightly fry the onions and peppers in the heated oil in the uncovered pressure cooker. Stir in the paprika and cook for 2–3 minutes. Add the garlic, tomatoes, stock and seasoning and mix well. Put the chicken joints on the vegetables, put on the lid and bring to high (15 lb) pressure. Cook for 4–6 minutes. Reduce pressure quickly. Put the chicken joints on a hot dish. Blend the cornflour to a smooth cream with a little cold water and stir a little of the hot cooking liquid. Add the mixture to the cooker and bring to the boil uncovered, stirring, and cook for about 2 minutes. Remove the cooker from the heat and stir in the yoghurt; mix well, adjust the seasoning and pour the sauce over the chicken.

Coq au vin

75 g (3 oz) streaky bacon rashers, rinded and
chopped
175 g (6 oz) mushrooms, sliced
8–12 small onions or shallots, skinned
15 ml (1 tbsp) oil
25 g (1 oz) butter
4 chicken joints
60 ml (4 tbsp) brandy
45 ml (3 level tbsp) flour
150 ml (¼ pint) chicken stock
300 ml (½ pint) red wine
bouquet garni
pinch of nutmeg
salt and pepper

Fry the bacon and vegetables in the heated oil and butter in the uncovered pressure cooker until they are well browned. Remove the bacon and vegetables and fry the chicken joints until they are well browned. Pour over the brandy and set light to it. When the flames have died down, remove the chicken and put it with the vegetables. Stir the flour into the remaining fat in the cooker and brown it. When it is well coloured, remove it from the cooker and put aside for use later. Return the vegetables and chicken to the cooker with the stock, red wine, bouquet garni, nutmeg and seasoning. Put on the lid and bring to high (15 lb) pressure. Cook for 4–6 minutes.

Reduce pressure quickly. Put the chicken and vegetables on a hot dish and remove the bouquet garni. Return the cooker to the heat, add the browned flour and bring to the boil uncovered, whisking until the sauce thickens. Adjust the seasoning and pour the sauce over the chicken and vegetables.

Coq au vin

Duck with orange

1 oven ready duck about 1·8–2 kg (4–4½ lb)
45 ml (3 level tbsp) seasoned flour
25 g (1 oz) butter or margarine
100 g (4 oz) button mushrooms
2 onions, skinned and chopped
1 large orange
300 ml (½ pint) stock made from the giblets
45 ml (3 tbsp) red wine
salt and pepper

Remove the skin and fat from the duck and put it with the giblets to make stock (see page 17). Strain the stock and leave the fat to settle, then skim off the fat before using.

Cut the duck into neat joints, sprinkle lightly with 30 ml (2 level tbsp) seasoned flour and fry the pieces in the fat in the uncovered pressure cooker. Remove the duck and fry the mushrooms and onions. Drain off any fat left in the cooker and return the duck joints. Thinly peel the orange with a potato peeler and finely slice the rind into small thin strips; put these in a small pan with a little water and simmer for about 5 minutes, until tender, then drain and leave to use later. Squeeze the juice from the orange and add it to the cooker with the stock, wine and seasoning. Put on the lid and bring to high (15 lb) pressure. Cook for 15 minutes. Reduce pressure quickly. Transfer the pieces of duck and the mushrooms to a hot casserole. Blend the remaining flour to a smooth cream with a little cold stock or red wine and stir in a little of the hot liquid. Add the mixture to the cooker and bring the sauce to the boil, stirring until

Beef and pepper casserole (see page 58) ▶

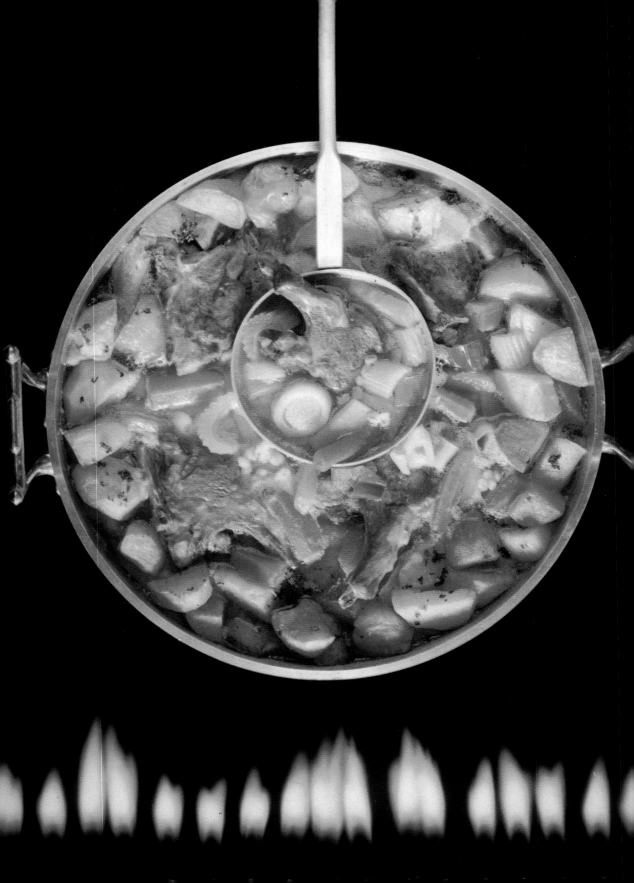

it thickens. Stir in the orange strips and pour the sauce over the duck.

Pork chops in cider

50 g (2 oz) butter
4 loin pork chops, well trimmed
2 crisp green eating apples, cored
300 ml (½ pint) cider
grated rind and juice of 1 lemon
salt and pepper
15 ml (1 level tbsp) cornflour

Melt the butter in the uncovered pressure cooker and quickly brown chops on both sides. Remove the meat from cooker. Cut the apples into 1-cm (½-in) slices and quickly fry them in the butter in the cooker until golden brown. Take out the apples and reserve. Return the chops to the cooker with the cider, lemon rind and seasoning. Put on lid and bring to high (15 lb) pressure. Cook for 12–15 minutes. Reduce pressure quickly. Place the chops on a hot dish and arrange the apple rings round them. Blend the cornflour to a smooth cream with a little water, add a little of the hot cooking liquid and add the mixture to the cooker with the lemon juice. Bring the sauce to the boil, stirring, and cook until it thickens. Pour the sauce over the chops and apples.

Barbecued pork chops

4 lean sparerib pork chops, trimmed
salt and pepper
15 ml (1 tbsp) cooking oil
30 ml (2 tbsp) clear honey
30 ml (2 tbsp) soy sauce
15 ml (1 tbsp) tomato ketchup
1 clove of garlic, skinned and crushed
1·25 ml (¼ level tsp) dry mustard
15–30 ml (1–2 tbsp) lemon juice
60 ml (4 tbsp) vinegar
1 small onion, skinned and chopped

Season the chops well. Heat the oil in the uncovered pressure cooker and fry the chops quickly until they are browned on both sides. Remove the meat from cooker and drain off the excess fat. Return the chops to the cooker. Mix the remaining ingredients, except the onions, to-gether in a bowl and add to the cooker with the onion. Put on the lid and bring to high (15 lb) pressure. Cook for 8–10 minutes. Reduce pressure quickly. Serve the chops with sauce spooned over them. Serve rice separately (see page 76).

Jugged hare

1 hare, jointed and with about 90 ml (6 tbsp) blood
30 ml (2 tbsp) oil
50 g (2 oz) streaky bacon, rinded and diced
3 onions, skinned and sliced
1 large carrot, pared and sliced
2 sticks of celery, washed, trimmed and chopped
salt and pepper
400 ml (¾ pint) stock (made from the hare giblets, head, heart, etc, see below)
30 ml (2 tbsp) lemon juice
bouquet garni
30 ml (2 level tbsp) flour
150 ml (¼ pint) port or red wine

For the forcemeat balls

100 g (4 oz) hare liver, sliced
50 g (2 oz) streaky bacon, rinded and chopped
1 onion, skinned and chopped
25 g (1 oz) butter or margarine
75 g (3 oz) fresh white breadcrumbs
10 ml (2 tbsp) chopped parsley
2·5 ml (½ level tsp) dried thyme
salt and pepper
1 egg, beaten
15–30 ml (1–2 tbsp) oil for frying

To make the forcemeat balls, lightly fry the hare liver with the bacon and onion in the fat in the uncovered pressure cooker. Finely chop the liver and mix with all other ingredients to a stiffish consistency. Form the mixture into small balls.

To make the stock, put the giblets, heart and head into the cooker with 600 ml (1 pint) water and seasoning. Put the lid on the cooker, bring to high (15 lb) pressure and cook for 20 minutes. Reduce pressure quickly and strain.

Fry the hare joints in the heated oil in the uncovered pressure cooker until well browned. Remove the hare and brown the prepared veget-ables. Take out the bacon and vegetables and drain off the excess fat. Return the hare and veget-ables to the cooker. Pour in the stock and lemon juice, add seasoning and the bouquet garni. Put

Lamb hotch potch (see page 59)

on the lid and bring to high (15 lb) pressure. Cook for 30–35 minutes (depending on the age of the hare). Meanwhile fry the forcemeat balls until well browned in a little hot oil. Reduce the cooker pressure quickly. Put the hare and vegetables in a hot casserole. Remove the bouquet garni and return the cooker to the heat. Blend the flour to a smooth cream with the wine and stir in a little of the hot cooking liquid. Add the mixture to the cooker, and bring the sauce to the boil, un-covered, stirring until it thickens. Adjust seasoning and remove the cooker from the heat. Stir in the reserved blood. Mix well and pour the sauce over the hare in the casserole. Garnish the hare with the forcemeat balls and serve with redcurrant jelly.

Rich rabbit casserole

The rabbit in this recipe is soaked overnight in cider, so start the preparation the day before cooking.

1 rabbit, jointed
300 ml (½ pint) dry cider
100 g (4 oz) prunes
50 g (2 oz) butter or margarine
8 small onions, skinned
100 g (4 oz) streaky bacon rashers, rinded and diced
30 ml (2 level tbsp) flour
150 ml (¼ pint) chicken or white stock
salt and pepper
bayleaf
1 large cooking apple

Put the rabbit joints in a deep casserole and pour over the cider. Leave to soak overnight. Pour boiling water to cover the prunes and soak for at least 10 minutes. Drain the cider from the rabbit and reserve. Wipe the rabbit with absorbent kitchen paper. Fry in the fat in the uncovered pressure cooker until it is well browned. Remove the rabbit and fry the onions and bacon. Take out the onions and bacon and sprinkle in the flour and cook until well browned; then remove it and keep it for use later. Return the rabbit, onions and bacon to the cooker. Pour in the stock, add the reserved cider,

strained prunes, seasoning and bayleaf. Put on the lid and bring to high (15 lb) pressure. Cook for 15 minutes. Reduce pressure quickly. Peel, core and slice the apple and add it to the cooker. Put on the lid and bring to high (15 lb) pressure. Cook for a further 5 minutes. Reduce pressure quickly. Put the rabbit, prunes, apples and onions in a hot dish and discard the bayleaf. Stir the browned flour into the hot cooking liquid and return the cooker to the heat. Bring to the boil uncovered, whisking until the gravy thickens. Adjust the seasoning and pour the sauce over the other ingredients.

Rabbit and onion blanquette

1 rabbit, jointed
100 g (4 oz) streaky bacon, rinded and chopped
1 large onion, skinned and studded with 3–4 cloves
bouquet garni
600 ml (1 pint) water
salt and pepper
6–8 small onions, skinned
25 g (1 oz) butter
30 ml (2 level tbsp) flour
300 ml (½ pint) milk
6–8 bacon rolls (see page 82)

Put the pieces of rabbit, bacon, large onion, bouquet garni and water in the pressure cooker with the well washed head of the rabbit and seasoning. Put on the lid and bring to high (15 lb) pressure. Cook for 12 minutes. Reduce pressure quickly. Remove the head, bouquet garni and onion and pour off 300 ml (½ pint) stock. Add the whole onions and put on the lid. Bring the cooker back to high (15 lb) pressure and cook for a further 6 minutes.

Meanwhile melt the butter in a saucepan and stir in flour. Remove the pan from the heat and gradually stir in the reserved stock and milk. Return pan to heat and bring to the boil, stirring, until the sauce thickens; cook for about 2 minutes. Remove the pressure cooker from the heat and reduce pressure quickly. Put the drained rabbit and onions in a casserole and pour over the sauce. Garnish with bacon rolls.

Pigeon and steak pudding

2 pigeons, plucked and drawn
225 g (8 oz) chuck steak
100 g (4 oz) steaky bacon, rinded and diced
2 medium-size onions, skinned and chopped
salt and pepper
400 ml (¾ pint) water
30 ml (2 tbsp) flour

For the suet crust pastry
225 g (8 oz) self raising flour
2·5 ml (½ level tsp) salt
100 g (4 oz) shredded suet
about 150 ml (¼ pint) cold water

Remove the flesh from the bones of the pigeon and cut it into 2·5-cm (1-in) pieces. Put it in the pressure cooker with the steak, cut into 2·5-cm (1-in) pieces, the bacon and the onions. Sprinkle with salt and pepper, pour in the water and put the pigeon bones on top. Cover with the lid and bring to high (15 lb) pressure. Cook for 15 minutes. Reduce pressure quickly.

Discard the pigeon bones. Blend the flour to a smooth cream with a little cold water and stir in some of the hot cooking liquid. Add the mixture to the cooker and bring to the boil uncovered, stirring until the liquid thickens. Adjust the seasoning, then leave to cool.

Make the suet crust pastry by mixing the dry ingredients to a soft dough with the water. Knead the dough on a floured surface, roll out three quarters of it and line a greased 900-ml (1½-pint) pudding basin. Roll the remaining pastry to form a lid. Spoon the cool pigeon mixture into the prepared basin with half the gravy (keep the rest to serve with the pudding later). Damp the pastry edges and fix on the pastry lid. Cover the basin with greased foil, tie a piece of string round the rim and over the top to form a handle.

Put 1·4 litres (2½ pints) water in the rinsed out pressure cooker, put in the trivet and bring the water to the boil. Lower the pudding on to the trivet. Put on the lid without the weight and lower the heat so that the cooker steams gently and steadily; leave to steam like this for 15 minutes. Then put on the weight and increase the heat to bring to low (5 lb) pressure. Cook for 30 minutes. Reduce the pressure slowly. Remove the pudding, and serve with the extra gravy, reheated.

Braised pigeons

2 young pigeons, drawn and trussed
15 ml (1 level tbsp) seasoned flour
30 ml (2 tbsp) oil
100 g (4 oz) streaky bacon rashers, rinded and diced
4 onions, skinned and sliced
4 sticks of celery, washed, trimmed, and sliced
salt and pepper
300 ml (½ pint) stock, made from the pigeon giblets
    if available
bouquet garni
1 orange
30 ml (2 level tbsp) flour
15 ml (1 level tbsp) redcurrant jelly

Dust the pigeons lightly with flour and fry them until brown in the oil, in the uncovered pressure cooker. Remove the pigeons and fry the bacon, onion and celery until they are well browned. Season and pour in the stock. Put pigeons on the vegetables, add the bouquet garni and put on the lid. Bring to high (15 lb) pressure. Cook for 20–25 minutes.

Meanwhile finely pare the orange rind with a potato peeler and cut into fine strips. Cook the rind for about 5 minutes in boiling water, then drain it. Squeeze the juice from the orange. Reduce the cooker pressure quickly. Put the pigeons and vegetables on a hot dish. Discard the bouquet garni and reheat the cooking liquid. Blend the flour to a smooth cream with the orange juice and stir in some of the hot liquid. Add the mixture to the cooker and bring the gravy to the boil uncovered, stirring until it thickens. Adjust the seasoning and stir in the orange rind and redcurrant jelly. Serve the pigeons with creamed potatoes and hand the gravy separately.
SERVES 2

Braised turkey legs

4 streaky bacon rashers, rinded
4 turkey drumsticks
30 ml (2 tbsp) oil
2 onions, skinned and quartered
2 carrots, pared and sliced
2 sticks of celery, washed, trimmed and chopped
100 g (4 oz) mushrooms, sliced
400 ml (¾ pint) stock
salt and pepper
bouquet garni
15 ml (1 level tbsp) tomato paste
30 ml (2 level tbsp) cornflour
15 ml (1 tbsp) chopped parsley

Wrap the bacon rashers round the drumsticks and fix in place with a cocktail stick. Fry the turkey in the heated oil in the pressure cooker until it is well browned. Remove the drumsticks and brown the prepared vegetables. Drain off the excess fat, stir in the stock, seasoning, bouquet garni and tomato paste. Put the turkey legs on the vegetables. Cover with the lid and bring to high (15 lb) pressure. Cook for 15 minutes. Reduce pressure quickly. Discard the bouquet garni and remove the cocktail sticks. Put the turkey and vegetables in a hot dish. Blend the cornflour to a smooth cream with a little cold water and stir in 30 ml (2 tbsp) of the hot liquid. Add the mixture to the cooker and bring to the boil uncovered, stirring until the gravy thickens. Pour the gravy over the turkey and serve sprinkled with parsley.

Ragoût of pigeon

2 pigeons, plucked, drawn and halved
30 ml (2 tbsp) oil
2 onions, skinned and sliced
100 g (4 oz) button mushrooms
100 g (4 oz) streaky bacon, rinded and diced
45 ml (3 level tbsp) flour
300 ml (½ pint) stock made from the giblets
150 ml (¼ pint) red wine
30 ml (2 level tbsp) tomato paste
bouquet garni
salt and pepper
50 g (2 oz) puff or flaky pastry, made weight, for fleurons

Fry the pigeons in the heated oil in the uncovered pressure cooker until brown. Remove the pigeons and fry the vegetables and bacon; drain well and put with the pigeons. Stir the flour into the remaining fat in the cooker and cook until well browned, then remove from cooker and keep for use later. Return the pigeons, vegetables, bacon, stock, wine, tomato paste, bouquet garni and seasoning. Put on the lid and bring to high (15 lb) pressure. Cook for 20–25 minutes, according to the age of the birds. Reduce pressure quickly. Put the pigeons and vegetables in a casserole. Remove the bouquet garni. Stir the browned flour into the remaining liquid and bring to the boil, whisking until the gravy thickens. Pour the sauce over the pigeons and serve garnished with pastry fleurons (see below).

Pastry fleurons

Roll out the pastry to about .5 cm (¼ in) thickness and cut it into crescents using a 2·5-cm (1-in) cutter. Put on a damp baking sheet and cook in the oven at 220°C (425°F) mark 7 for about 5 minutes until brown and crisp.

Veal goulash

450 g (1 lb) pie veal, cut into cubes
25 g (1 oz) lard
1 large onion, skinned and sliced
1 large green pepper, seeded and sliced
30 ml (2 level tbsp) paprika pepper
226-g (8-oz) can of tomatoes
300 ml (½ pint) chicken stock
pinch of nutmeg
2·5 ml (½ level tsp) dried sage, optional
salt
freshly ground pepper
15 ml (1 level tbsp) cornflour
142-ml (5-fl oz) carton of soured cream, stirred

Fry the veal in the fat in the uncovered pressure cooker until it is well browned. Remove the meat from the cooker. Add the onion and pepper and cook until the onion is soft. Stir in the paprika and cook for 1 minute. Add the tomatoes with juice, stock, nutmeg, sage, salt and pepper. Return the meat to the cooker. Put on the lid and bring to high (15 lb) pressure. Cook for 20 minutes. Reduce pressure quickly. Blend the cornflour to a smooth cream with a little cold water and stir in a little of the cooking liquid. Add the mixture to cooker, bring to the boil uncovered, stirring until the sauce thickens. Serve with soured cream and boiled rice (see page 76).

Ragoût of ox heart with lemon

450 g (1 lb) ox heart
25 g (1 oz) butter or margarine
1 medium-size onion, skinned and sliced
400 ml (¾ pint) stock
10 ml (2 level tsp) grated lemon rind
5 ml (1 tsp) lemon juice
2·5 ml (½ level tsp) mixed dried herbs
salt and pepper
15 ml (1 level tbsp) flour
150-ml (5-fl oz) carton of soured cream, stirred
15 ml (1 tbsp) chopped parsley

Trim the heart, discard any pipes or gristle, and cut the meat into 1-cm (½-in) strips. Melt the fat in the uncovered pressure cooker and fry the strips of heart until brown. Remove the heart and fry the onion lightly. Return the meat to cooker with the stock, lemon rind and juice, herbs and seasoning. Put on the lid and bring to high (15 lb) pressure. Cook for 20 minutes. Reduce pressure quickly. Blend the flour to a smooth cream with a little cold water and stir in 45 ml (3 tbsp) of the hot liquid. Add the mixture to the cooker and bring the sauce to the boil uncovered, stirring until it thickens. Stir in the soured cream, adjust the seasoning and serve sprinkled with parsley.

Braised oxtail

1 oxtail, jointed
30 ml (2 tbsp) oil
3 onions, skinned and sliced
1 small head of celery, washed, trimmed and chopped
425-g (15-oz) can of tomatoes
bouquet garni
400 ml (¾ pint) stock
150 ml (¼ pint) red wine
salt and pepper
30 ml (2 level tbsp) flour
15 ml (1 tbsp) chopped parsley

Trim excess fat from the oxtail and fry it in the hot

oil in the uncovered pressure cooker until it is well browned. Remove the meat and brown the onions and celery. Drain off excess fat. Add the tomatoes with juice, bouquet garni, stock and wine. Season well. Put the oxtail joints on top. Put on the lid and bring to high (15 lb) pressure. Cook for 35–40 minutes (depending on the size of the joints). Reduce pressure quickly. Put the oxtail and vegetables in a hot dish and discard bouquet garni. Blend the flour to a smooth cream with a little cold water and stir in a little of the hot liquid. Add the mixture to the cooker and bring the gravy to the boil uncovered, stirring until it thickens. Adjust the seasoning. Pour the gravy over the oxtail and serve sprinkled with parsley.

Osso bucco

1 kg (2¼ lb) shin of veal
salt and pepper
50 g (2 oz) butter or margarine
1 large onion, skinned and sliced
1 large carrot, pared and thinly sliced
1 large clove of garlic, skinned and crushed
bouquet garni
225 g (8 oz) tomatoes, skinned and chopped
15 ml (1 level tbsp) tomato paste
150 ml (¼ pint) dry white wine
400 ml (¾ pint) white stock
30 ml (2 level tbsp) cornflour
15 ml (1 tbsp) chopped parsley
10 ml (2 level tsp) grated lemon rind

Have the veal cut into 3-cm (1¼-in) pieces. Season the meat with salt and pepper and fry in the fat in the uncovered pressure cooker until it is well browned. Remove the meat and fry the onion and carrot until brown. Drain off the excess fat and return the veal to the cooker with the garlic, bouquet garni, tomatoes, tomato paste, wine, stock and a little extra seasoning. Put on the lid and bring to high (15 lb) pressure. Cook for 20 minutes. Reduce pressure quickly. Put the meat and vegetables in a hot dish. Return the cooker to the heat. Blend the cornflour to a smooth cream with a little cold water, and stir in 30 ml (2 tbsp) of the hot liquid. Add the mixture to the cooker and bring the gravy to the boil uncovered, stirring until it thickens. Adjust the seasoning and pour the gravy over the veal. Sprinkle with the parsley and grated lemon rind before serving.

Mexican liver

450 g (1 lb) lamb's liver
15 ml (1 level tbsp) seasoned flour
50 g (2 oz) fat or oil
2 onions, skinned and sliced
250 g (8 oz) tomatoes, skinned and quartered
1 red pepper, seeded and sliced
salt and pepper
300 ml (½ pint) stock
30 ml (2 level tbsp) cornflour

Wash and dry the liver and cut it into 1-cm (½-in) slices. Toss it in the seasoned flour and fry lightly in the oil in the uncovered pressure cooker over low heat until the liver is just sealed. Take out the liver and fry the onions, tomatoes and red pepper. Drain off any fat, and return the liver to the cooker with seasoning and stock. Put on the lid and bring to high (15 lb) pressure. Cook for 4 minutes. Reduce pressure quickly. Put the liver and vegetables in a hot casserole and keep it warm. Blend the cornflour to a smooth cream with a little cold water and stir in some of the hot stock. Add the mixture to the cooker and bring the gravy to the boil uncovered, stirring until it thickens. Pour the gravy over the liver mixture. Serve with creamed potatoes and a green vegetable.

Casserole of lambs' tongues

4 lambs' tongues
2 medium-size onions, skinned and chopped
50 g (2 oz) butter or margarine
60 ml (4 level tbsp) flour
1 carrot, pared and sliced
3–4 sticks of celery, washed, trimmed and chopped
4 medium-size tomatoes, skinned and quartered
bouquet garni
300 ml (½ pint) stock
salt and pepper
30 ml (2 level tbsp) tomato paste

Trim and wash the tongues. Lightly fry the onions in the fat in the uncovered pressure cooker until golden brown, then remove them. Sprinkle in the flour and cook until it is brown. Remove the browned flour to use later. Put the tongues, vegetables, tomatoes, bouquet garni, stock and seasoning in the pressure cooker. Put on the lid and bring to high (15 lb) pressure. Cook for 30 minutes. Reduce pressure quickly. Skin the tongues and remove any bones and gristle from the thick ends. Put the tongues and vegetables in a hot dish and keep them warm. Remove the bouquet garni. Add the browned flour to the stock, stir in the tomato paste, return the cooker to the heat and bring the contents to the boil uncovered, whisking until the gravy thickens. Adjust the seasoning then pour the gravy into the casserole.

Stuffed lambs' hearts

4 small lambs' hearts
30 ml (2 level tbsp) seasoned flour
25 g (1 oz) fat or oil
1 onion, skinned and sliced
1 carrot, pared and chopped
4 sticks of celery, washed, trimmed and sliced
400 ml (¾ pint) stock
salt and pepper
30 ml (2 level tbsp) flour

For the stuffing

100 g (4 oz) fresh white breadcrumbs
1 medium-size onion, skinned and finely chopped
45 ml (3 tbsp) melted butter
10 ml (2 level tsp) mixed dried herbs
salt and pepper
1 small egg, beaten

Mix together the stuffing ingredients and bind with the egg. Wash the hearts and remove any tubes or gristle with kitchen scissors. Make a good opening for the stuffing, wash and dry well. Spoon the stuffing into the hearts and stitch together with fine string. Roll the hearts in the seasoned flour and brown them in hot fat in the uncovered pressure cooker. Remove the hearts and fry the prepared vegetables. Drain off any fat and return the hearts to the cooker with the stock and seasoning. Put on the lid and bring to high (15 lb) pressure. Cook for 25 minutes. Reduce pressure quickly. Remove the hearts and vegetables and place them in a hot dish: keep it warm. Mix the flour to a smooth cream with a little cold water and stir in a little of the hot stock. Add the mixture to the cooker, return the cooker to the heat and bring the contents to the boil, stirring until the gravy thickens. Adjust the seasoning and pour the gravy over the hearts. Serve with creamed potatoes.

Pork balls with rice

75 g (3 oz) fresh white breadcrumbs
150 ml (¼ pint) milk
225 g (8 oz) pie veal, minced
225 g (8 oz) lean pork, minced
1 egg, beaten
salt
freshly ground pepper
700 ml (1¼ pints) stock
1 large onion, skinned and quartered
1 large carrot, pared and sliced
1 stick of celery, washed, trimmed and chopped
bouquet garni
250 g (8 oz) long grain rice
fresh tomato sauce (see page 81)

Soak the breadcrumbs in the milk. Mix together the minced meats, the egg and the seasoning. Add the soaked breadcrumbs and work the mixture until it is smooth (it will be fairly soft). Shape it into about twenty balls. Put the stock, vegetables and bouquet garni in the pressure cooker and bring to the boil. Add the meat balls, put on the lid and bring to high (15 lb) pressure. Cook for 4 minutes. Reduce pressure quickly. Transfer the pork balls to a hot dish and keep warm. Strain the stock and return 600 ml (1 pint) to the cooker. Bring the stock to the boil and stir in the rice. Put on the lid and bring to high (15 lb) pressure. Cook for 5 minutes. Reduce pressure slowly. Strain the rice and serve it with the pork balls and tomato sauce.

Kidneys in red wine

8 lambs' kidneys
100 g (4 oz) streaky bacon, rinded and diced
25 g (1 oz) butter or margarine
1 large onion, skinned and sliced
45 ml (3 level tbsp) seasoned flour
100 g (4 oz) button mushrooms
300 ml (½ pint) stock
salt and pepper
15 ml (1 level tbsp) tomato paste
150 ml (¼ pint) red wine

Skin, core and halve the kidneys. Lightly fry the bacon in the fat in the uncovered pressure cooker until it is just brown and some of the fat has run out. Remove the bacon from the cooker and lightly fry the onions until they are just transparent. Remove the onion and put with the bacon. Toss the kidneys in the seasoned flour, shake off most of it, and fry them in the uncovered cooker until just sealed. Put the bacon, onion, mushrooms and stock in the cooker. Add the seasoning, tomato paste and wine. Put on the lid and bring to high (15 lb) pressure. Cook for 5 minutes. Reduce pressure quickly. Spoon the kidneys and vegetables into a hot dish and keep it warm. Blend the remaining flour to a smooth cream with a little cold water and stir in a little of the hot stock. Add the mixture to the cooker and bring the sauce to the boil uncovered, stirring until it thickens. Adjust the seasoning and pour the sauce over the kidneys. Serve with creamed potatoes or rice.

Lancashire tripe and onions

700 g (1½ lb) dressed tripe
225 g (8 oz) onions, skinned and sliced
300 ml (½ pint) stock or water
salt and pepper
bayleaf
6–8 shallots, skinned
25 g (1 oz) butter or margarine
45 ml (3 level tbsp) flour
150 ml (¼ pint) milk
15 ml (1 tbsp) chopped parsley
toast triangles for garnish

Cut the tripe into 5-cm (2-in) pieces. Put it in the pressure cooker with the sliced onions, stock, seasoning and bayleaf. Put on the lid and bring to high (15 lb) pressure. Cook for 7 minutes. Reduce pressure quickly. Put the shallots in a vegetable separator and sprinkle with salt. Put the trivet over the tripe and stand the separator on it. Put on the lid and bring to high (15 lb) pressure. Cook for a further 3 minutes. Reduce pressure quickly. Put the tripe and shallots in a hot dish.

Meanwhile melt the fat in a saucepan, stir in the flour and cook it for 2–3 minutes. Remove the pan from heat and gradually stir in 150 ml (¼ pint) cooking liquid and 150 ml (¼ pint) milk. Return the pan to heat and bring the sauce to the boil, stirring until it thickens. Add the tripe and shallots to the sauce to reheat, adjust seasoning and serve sprinkled with parsley and garnished with triangles of toast.

Beef curry

See colour picture facing page 80.

2 medium-size onions, skinned and chopped
45 ml (3 tbsp) oil
15 ml (1 level tbsp) ground coriander
15 ml (1 level tbsp) ground cummin
5 ml (1 level tsp) ground turmeric
small pinch of chilli powder
small pinch of ground ginger
pinch of ground cinnamon
2·5 ml (½ level tsp) ground clove
2·5 ml (½ level tsp) fenugreek
30 ml (2 tbsp) vinegar
15 ml (1 tbsp) lemon juice
700 g (1½ lb) chuck steak, cut into 2·5-cm (1-in) cubes
bayleaf
1 clove of garlic, skinned and crushed
396-g (14-oz) can of tomatoes
300 ml (½ pint) stock
salt and pepper
225 g (8 oz) long grain rice
600 ml (1 pint) salted water

Note: Instead of the spices listed above, from coriander to fenugreek inclusive, 45 ml (3 level tbsp) curry powder may be used.

Fry the onions in the heated oil in the uncovered pressure cooker, until soft and transparent. Mix together the curry spices and blend to a paste with the vinegar and lemon juice. Stir the mixture into the onions and leave to cook for about 5 minutes, stirring frequently to bring out the spice flavours. Stir in the diced meat and continue to cook uncovered until it is well mixed with the spices. Add the bayleaf, garlic, and tomatoes with the juice, stock and seasoning. Put on the lid and bring to high (15 lb) pressure. Cook for 15 minutes.

Meanwhile put the rice in a greased solid separator or ovenproof dish. Pour on the salted water. Cover with a piece of greased foil. Reduce the cooker pressure quickly. Place the trivet on the curry and stand the dish of rice on top. Put on the lid and bring to high (15 lb) pressure. Cook for a further 5 minutes. Reduce pressure slowly.

Flake the rice with a fork and serve it with the curry.

Suggestions for side dishes
Poppadums, mango chutney, sliced bananas with lemon juice, sliced red or green peppers with French dressing, sliced skinned tomatoes with French dressing, diced cucumber and yoghurt, sliced peeled oranges and onion rings.

Ragoût of venison

The venison in this recipe is marinaded for up to 12 hours, so start the preparation in advance.

700 g (1½ lb) shoulder of venison or other stewing part
1 clove of garlic, skinned and crushed
salt and freshly ground pepper
1 large bayleaf
10 ml (2 tsp) vinegar
150 ml (¼ pint) red wine
100 g (4 oz) streaky bacon rashers, rinded and diced
50 g (2 oz) butter or margarine
2 onions, skinned and sliced
2 large carrots, pared and sliced
45 ml (3 level tbsp) flour
300 ml (½ pint) stock

Cut the meat into 5-cm (2-in) cubes and put it in a deep dish. Mix together the garlic, seasoning, bayleaf, vinegar and wine and pour it over the venison. Leave to marinade for up to 12 hours, stirring frequently.

Strain the marinade and reserve it. Pat the meat dry, using a piece of absorbent kitchen paper. Lightly fry the bacon in the fat in the uncovered pressure cooker, then remove it and fry the meat until it is well browned. Remove the meat, fry the vegetables then put them with the meat. Sprinkle the flour into the remaining fat in the cooker and brown it, then take it out of cooker to use later. Return the meat, bacon and vegetables to the cooker, adding seasoning, the marinade liquid and the stock. Put on the lid and bring to high (15 lb) pressure. Cook for 20 minutes. Reduce pressure quickly. Add the browned flour, return the cooker to the heat and bring the contents to the boil uncovered, whisking until the ragoût thickens. Adjust the seasoning and serve with creamed potatoes and redcurrant jelly.

PULSES, PASTA AND RICE

Although pulses, cereals and pasta have always been used for certain dishes they have never played a very important part in diet in our affluent society. Now that meat, fish and other foods are increasing in price, pulses, pasta and cereals are becoming a delicious and filling booster to a meal.

The pulses, which include the bean and pea families, are high in protein and therefore can be used to replace or supplement some of the more expensive proteins. Normally they require over-night soaking and long cooking to make them tender. A pressure cooker will dramatically reduce the cooking time, which makes them even more economical, and cuts out the long soaking.

Pastas, which come in a variety of shapes and sizes, are made from hard semolina wheat which also contains protein. They make a good basis for a quick meal and are usually served with a savoury sauce and grated cheese. As a general rule, pastas require about a third of the normal cooking time when pressure cooked, although the cooking time does vary with the type of pasta.

Rice, barley and oatmeal are the cereals most generally used. The specially processed quick cooking varieties, however, do not require pres-sure cooking and are best cooked according to the manufacturer's instructions. But the cooking time for untreated cereals can be reduced by

using a pressure cooker. Rice, for example, cooks in about a third of the usual time.

General instructions for cooking pulses in the pressure cooker

First pick over the pulses, to remove any stones, and wash them. Soak all pulses, except lentils, for at least 1 hour before use. To do this, pour over boiling water and leave them to soak in the hot water. Then follow instructions according to the recipe or:

1. Remove the trivet from cooker and put in the water. Allow at least 1·1 litre (2 pints) fresh cold water to every 450 g (1 lb) pulse.

2. Never have the cooker more than half full.

3. Bring the water to boiling point and add the pulses, with seasonings. Allow to come to the boil again, uncovered, stirring frequently to prevent them sticking on the base, and remove any scum.

4. Put on the lid, lower the heat so that the contents boil gently and bring to high (15 lb) pressure.

5. Cook for the required time according to the chart.

6. Remove cooker from heat and reduce pressure slowly as the pulses are liable to rise and block the vent if the pressure is reduced quickly.

7. Drain pulses and use as required.

8. Wash the cooker and lid thoroughly to ensure the vent is clean and unblocked.

Guide to pressure cooking pulses

	Cooking time at high (15 lb) pressure	How to reduce pressure		Cooking time at high (15 lb) pressure	How to reduce pressure
Lentils	15 minutes	slowly	Haricot beans	20 minutes	slowly
Split peas	15 minutes	slowly	Red kidney beans	20 minutes	slowly
Whole peas or			Blackeye beans	20 minutes	slowly
chick peas	20 minutes	slowly	Butter beans	20 minutes	slowly
Flageolet beans	20 minutes	slowly			

Beef and bean casserole

175 g (6 oz) red kidney beans
350 g (12 oz) stewing beef
30 ml (2 tbsp) oil
2 large onions, skinned and sliced
1 medium green pepper about 100 g (4 oz), washed, seeded and sliced
2·5 ml (½ level tsp) dried thyme
15 ml (1 level tbsp) Worcestershire sauce
salt and pepper
300 ml (½ pint) stock
30 ml (2 level tbsp) flour

Wash the beans, pour boiling water over them and leave to soak for at least 1 hour. Trim the beef and cut it into 2·5-cm (1-in) cubes. Fry the meat in the heated oil in the uncovered pressure cooker until it is well browned. Remove the meat and fry the onions lightly with the pepper. Return the meat to the cooker with the beans, thyme, Worcestershire sauce seasonings and stock. Put on the lid and bring to high (15 lb) pressure. Cook for 20 minutes. Reduce pressure slowly. Blend the flour to a smooth cream with a little cold water, then stir in a little of the hot cooking liquid. Add the mixture to the cooker and stir until the liquid thickens and boils. Adjust seasoning and serve with green salad or a vegetable.

Bean and tomato salad

175 g (6 oz) red kidney or flageolet beans
2·5 ml (½ level tsp) dry mustard
1·25 ml (¼ level tsp) salt
1·25 ml (¼ level tsp) freshly ground pepper
5 ml (1 level tsp) sugar
1 clove of garlic, skinned and crushed
30–45 ml (2–3 tbsp) olive oil
30 ml (2 tbsp) vinegar
2–3 stalks of celery, trimmed and washed
1 medium-size dessert apple, peeled and cored
50 g (2 oz) chopped walnuts
oz) chopped walnuts
4 firm tomatoes, skinned and deseeded
2 lettuce hearts

Wash the beans, pour boiling water over them and leave to soak for at least 1 hour. Put the drained beans in the pressure cooker with 600 ml (1 pint) water containing 10 ml (2 level tsp) salt. Put on the lid and bring to high (15 lb) pressure. Cook for 20 minutes. Reduce pressure slowly. Strain off the

water and leave the beans to cool. Put the mustard, salt, pepper and sugar in a bowl, add the garlic and oil. Gradually mix in the vinegar and test for seasoning. Spoon a little of the dressing over the beans while they are cooling.

Cut the celery into 2·5-cm (1-in) thin strips, cut the apple into 1-cm (½-in) cubes and mix with the walnuts and rest of the dressing. Cut the tomato flesh into 1-cm (½-in) dice and gently stir into the other ingredients, and lastly stir in the beans. Arrange lettuce hearts on a dish and spoon the bean and tomato salad into the centre. Serve as a winter salad with cold meats or fish.

Cassoulet

The salt pork in this recipe has to be soaked for up to 12 hours, so start the preparation the day before you cook the dish.

225 g (8 oz) haricot beans
225 g (8 oz) streaky salt pork, soaked for up to 12 hours
225 g (8 oz) boned shoulder of lamb
8 medium-size onions, skinned and sliced
25 g (1 oz) lard
600 ml (1 pint) stock
1 large clove of garlic, skinned and crushed
30 ml (2 level tbsp) tomato paste
100 g (4 oz) garlic sausage, sliced
5 ml (1 level tsp) sugar
bayleaf
salt and freshly ground pepper
100 g (4 oz) fried crumbs

Wash the beans and pour boiling water over them; leave to soak for at least 1 hour. Drain well. Remove the rind from the pork and cut the meat into strips. Remove excess fat from the lamb and cut the lamb into similar sized pieces. Fry the onions in the hot fat in the uncovered pressure cooker, then fry the meats until browned. Pour in the stock and add the beans, garlic, tomato paste, sliced sausage, sugar, bayleaf and seasoning. Cover with the lid and bring to high (15 lb) pressure. Cook for 20 minutes. Reduce pressure slowly. Spoon the contents of cooker into a hot casserole; sprinkle with a layer of fried crumbs before serving.

Fried crumbs

Melt 50 g (2 oz) butter in a frying pan over gentle

heat. Stir in 100 g (4 oz) fresh white breadcrumbs and cook, stirring until they are all golden brown and crisp.

Chilli con carne

175 g (6 oz) red kidney beans
15 ml (1 tbsp) oil
450 g (1 lb) minced beef
1 large onion, skinned and chopped
30 ml (2 level tbsp) tomato paste
10 ml (2 level tsp) chilli seasoning
1 clove of garlic, skinned and crushed
1·25 ml (¼ level tsp) cayenne pepper
396-g (14-oz) can of tomatoes
150 ml (¼ pint) beef stock
salt and freshly ground pepper

Wash the beans, pour boiling water over them and leave to soak for at least 1 hour. Heat oil in the uncovered pressure cooker, add the beef and quickly brown. Add the onion and continue cooking for 2 minutes. Stir in the tomato paste, chilli seasoning, garlic, cayenne pepper, tomatoes with the juice, drained beans, stock, and bring to the boil. Adjust seasoning. Put the lid on the cooker and bring up to high (15 lb) pressure. Cook for 20 minutes. Reduce pressure slowly.
Note: Do not use ground chilli or chilli powder. The American chilli seasoning used in this recipe is a milder pre-mixed seasoning based on ground Mexican chilli, so try to use this type.

Chick pea sambal

This is a good accompaniment to meat curry.

250 g (8 oz) chick peas
1 medium-size onion, skinned and sliced
50 g (2 oz) butter
5 ml (1 level tsp) ground cummin
2·5 ml (½ level tsp) ground ginger
5 ml (1 level tsp) ground coriander
pinch of chilli powder
1 medium-size potato, peeled and diced
300 ml (½ pint) water or stock
salt and pepper
good squeeze of lemon juice

Wash the peas, pour boiling water over them and leave to soak for at least 1 hour. Fry the onion in the melted butter in the uncovered cooker until just

transparent, then fry the spices. Add the potato and cook for a few minutes. Put the drained peas in the cooker with the water or stock, seasoning and lemon juice. Put on lid; bring to high (15 lb) pressure. Cook for 20 minutes. Reduce pressure slowly.

Indian dahl

This is a good accompaniment to curry.

1 medium-size onion, skinned and chopped
50 g (2 oz) butter
15 ml (1 level tbsp) curry powder
100 g (4 oz) lentils, washed
400 ml (¾ pint) stock
5 ml (1 level tsp) salt
freshly ground pepper

Fry the onion in the melted butter in the uncovered pressure cooker until tender and just brown, then fry the curry powder. Stir in the lentils and mix well so that they are well covered with fat. Add the stock and seasoning. Stir well and bring to the boil uncovered, then stir again. Put on the lid and bring to high (15 lb) pressure. Cook for 15 minutes. Reduce pressure slowly. Remove the lid and continue to cook over gentle heat, stirring all the time until a thick purée is formed Adjust the seasoning and pile the dahl into a hot dish.

Lentil stew

2 medium-size onions, skinned and sliced
100 g (4 oz) mushrooms, sliced
2 sticks of celery, trimmed, washed and diced
50 g (2 oz) butter
175 g (6 oz) lentils, washed
226-g (8-oz) can of tomatoes
600 ml (1 pint) vegetable stock or water
1 clove of garlic, skinned and crushed
5 ml (1 level tsp) salt
freshly ground pepper
5 ml (1 level tsp) Marmite
25 g (1 oz) mature Cheddar cheese, grated
25 g (1 oz) fried breadcrumbs (see page 74)

Fry the onions, mushrooms and celery in the melted butter in the uncovered pressure cooker until lightly browned. Stir in the lentils and mix well to ensure they are well coated with fat. Add the tomatoes with the juice, stock, garlic, seasoning and Marmite. Put on the lid and bring to high (15 lb) pressure. Cook for 15 minutes. Reduce pressure slowly. Adjust seasoning and put the mixture into an ovenproof casserole. Mix together the cheese and crumbs, sprinkle them thickly over the top of the stew and brown under the grill.

Lentil and nut burgers

2 medium-size onions, skinned and finely
    chopped
100 g (4 oz) mushrooms, finely chopped
50 g (2 oz) butter
150 g (6 oz) lentils
600 ml (1 pint) vegetable stock
bouquet garni
salt and pepper
2 eggs, separated
75 g (3 oz) mixed nuts (walnuts, hazel, almonds),
    finely chopped
50–100 g (2–4 oz) fresh white breadcrumbs
vegetable oil for frying

Fry the onions and mushrooms in the melted butter in the uncovered cooker for 2–3 minutes until just brown. Stir in the lentils so that they are well coated with fat. Add the stock, bouquet garni and seasoning. Stir well, then put on the lid and bring to high (15 lb) pressure. Cook for 15 minutes. Reduce pressure slowly. Take out the bouquet garni. Continue to cook the mixture over gentle heat in the uncovered cooker, stirring well until the mixture has dried out and is fairly firm. Stir in the egg yolks and nuts and adjust the seasoning. Turn the mixture on to a floured board and shape into six to eight flat cakes. Dip each cake into the lightly whisked egg whites, then into the crumbs to make a coating. Heat the oil in a frying pan until just hot and fry the burgers until brown on both sides. Serve with tomato sauce (see page 81).

General instructions for cooking rice in the pressure cooker

Cooking long grain rice on its own
1. Remove the trivet from the pressure cooker and put in 1·1 litres (2 pints) water and 15 ml (1 level tbsp) salt, bring to the boil.
2. Throw in 225 g (8 oz) washed long grain rice and stir well to ensure that the grains are not sticking to the base of the pan. (Allow about 50 g (2 oz) rice per person if served as an accompaniment to a dish.)

Note : Never fill the pressure cooker more than half full: 225 g (8 oz) of rice is about the maximum to cook at one time.

3. Put on the lid and bring to high (15 lb) pressure, keeping the heat a little lower than usual as the rice is apt to froth up if it cooks too quickly. Cook for 5 minutes.
4. Should the contents froth up and spurt through the vent, remove the cooker from the heat and allow the contents to subside. Wipe round the vent with a damp cloth and make sure it is clear. Slowly bring to pressure again.
5. Reduce pressure quickly, and remove lid.
6. Strain the rice through a fine sieve and run boiling water over it. Put in a hot dish and keep hot until required, stirring now and again with a fork.
7. Wash the cooker thoroughly, making sure the vent is clean and unblocked.

Cooking long grain rice with other foods
1. Put 225 g (8 oz) washed long grain rice in the solid separator of the pressure cooker or in an ovenproof dish, well buttered.
2. Pour on 600 ml (1 pint) cold water and 5 ml (1 level tsp) salt. Cover with a piece of greased foil.
3. Stand the container on the trivet on top of the food already in the pressure cooker.
4. Bring to high (15 lb) pressure and cook for 5 minutes.
5. Reduce pressure slowly. Fluff the rice with a fork before putting it in a hot dish. If wished, the rice can be dried a little in a moderate oven before serving.

Milanese risotto

1 medium-size onion, skinned and chopped
50 g (2 oz) butter
225 g (8 oz) long grain rice
150 ml (¼ pint) dry white wine
400 ml (¾ pint) chicken stock
salt and pepper
pinch of saffron powder
30 ml (2 tbsp) stock
Parmesan cheese or other hard cheese, grated

Fry the onion in the melted butter in the uncovered pressure cooker until it is just soft and golden. Stir in the rice and continue to cook until all the fat has been absorbed but do not let the rice brown. Pour in the wine and stock, add the seasoning and bring to the boil uncovered; stir well. Put on the lid and bring to high (15 lb) pressure. Cook for 7 minutes. Reduce the pressure slowly. Meanwhile soak the saffron powder in 30 ml (2 tbsp) stock for about 5 minutes. Strain the saffron into the rice mixture and continue to heat gently in the uncovered cooker until the risotto is dry again. Adjust the seasoning. Serve the risotto piled on a hot dish with plenty of grated cheese (preferably Parmesan).

Lamb pilau

3 medium-size onions, skinned
700 g (1 ½ lb) best end of neck of lamb
1 clove of garlic, skinned and crushed
salt and pepper
600 ml (1 pint) water
30 ml (2 tbsp) oil
25 g (1 oz) butter
2·5 ml (½ level tsp) ground cinnamon
pinch of ground cloves
225 g (8 oz) long grain rice
50 g (2 oz) raisins

Chop two onions finely and slice the third one. Trim off excess fat from the meat and cut into cutlets. Put the trivet in the pressure cooker and stand the cutlets on it with the sliced onion, garlic, and seasoning. Pour on the water, put on the lid and bring to high (15 lb) pressure. Cook for 10 minutes. Reduce pressure quickly. Strain off stock, making it up to 600 ml (1 pint) if necessary with water. Remove the trivet and rinse out the cooker. Heat the oil and butter in the uncovered cooker and fry the cutlets until they have just browned, then remove them and keep hot. Fry the chopped onions, cinnamon and cloves for a few minutes in the remaining fat until the onions are just transparent. Then stir in the rice and cook it until all fat has been absorbed. Remove the cooker from the heat, stir in the stock, raisins and salt and pepper. Put on the lid and bring to high (15 lb) pressure. Cook for 7 minutes. Reduce the pressure quickly.

Stir the rice well and pile it on a hot dish with the cutlets in the centre.

Spanish rice

100 g (4 oz) streaky bacon rashers, rinded and chopped
25 g (1 oz) butter
1 medium-size onion, skinned and chopped
1 green pepper, seeded and sliced
225 g (8 oz) long grain rice
1 clove of garlic, skinned and crushed
600 ml (1 pint) chicken stock
4 medium-size tomatoes, skinned and chopped
salt and pepper
pinch of sugar

Lightly fry the bacon in the butter in the uncovered pressure cooker until the fat runs out and the bacon browns slightly. Remove bacon from the cooker and fry the onion and pepper. Stir in the rice and cook for 2–3 minutes, then add the garlic, stock, tomatoes, salt and pepper. Sprinkle in the sugar and return the bacon to the cooker. Bring the contents to the boil uncovered, stirring to prevent the rice sticking. Put on the lid and bring to high (15 lb) pressure. Cook for 7 minutes. Reduce pressure quickly. Adjust the seasoning and serve piled on a hot dish as an accompaniment to boiled chicken or rabbit.

Risotto with mussels

2·3 litres (4 pints) mussels
2 medium-size onions, skinned and chopped
1 clove of garlic, skinned and crushed
1 stick of celery, washed, trimmed and chopped
300 ml (½ pint) dry white wine
bouquet garni
4 peppercorns
50 g (2 oz) butter
225 g (8 oz) long grain rice
salt and pepper
grated Parmesan cheese

Wash and scrub the mussels and discard any that are broken, open or cracked. Put them in the pressure cooker with 1 onion, the garlic, celery, wine, bouquet garni and peppercorns. (Take care not to have the cooker more than half full.) Put on the lid and bring to high (15 lb) pressure.

Cook for 1 minute. Reduce pressure quickly, strain off the liquid and reserve. Remove the mussels from the shells and keep aside.

Lightly fry the other onion in the butter in the rinsed cooker, uncovered, until just transparent and lightly coloured. Stir in the rice and cook for 2–3 minutes without browning, then stir in 600 ml (1 pint) mussel stock. Bring to the boil, stirring well to prevent the rice sticking to the base. Put on the lid and bring to high (15 lb) pressure. Cook for 7 minutes. Reduce pressure quickly. Stir in the mussels and adjust the seasoning. Reheat gently, stirring with a fork until all the liquid has been absorbed. Pile on to a hot dish and serve with grated Parmesan cheese.

Cheese and rice pudding

3 medium-size onions, skinned
50 g (2 oz) long grain rice
5 ml (1 level tsp) salt
400 ml (¾ pint) milk
freshly ground pepper
5 ml (1 level tsp) made mustard
1 egg, beaten
75 g (3 oz) mature cheese, grated
50 g (2 oz) butter or margarine
50 g (2 oz) small mushrooms, sliced
15 ml (1 tbsp) chopped parsley

Put 300 ml (½ pint) water in the pressure cooker with the trivet. Chop one onion and slice the others. Put the rice and the chopped onion in an 18-cm (7-in) soufflé dish and sprinkle with salt. Pour on the milk and stand the dish on the trivet. Cover lightly with foil. Put on the lid and bring to high (15 lb) pressure. Cook for 5 minutes. Reduce pressure slowly. Stir the pepper, mustard, egg and cheese into the rice mixture and mix well. Cover with foil again, put on the lid and bring to high (15 lb) pressure and cook for a further 2 minutes. Reduce pressure slowly.

Meanwhile fry the two sliced onions in the fat in a frying pan. When they are golden and nearly cooked, add the mushrooms and cook for a further 2–3 minutes. Lastly, stir in the parsley. Remove the rice dish from the cooker, arrange the onion mixture on top and serve with crusty bread and butter.

Risotto with chicken livers

50 g (2 oz) butter
15 ml (1 tbsp) oil
1 medium-size onion, skinned and chopped
50 g (2 oz) mushrooms, chopped
225 g (8 oz) chicken livers
15 ml (1 level tbsp) seasoned flour
225 g (8 oz) long grain rice
600 ml (1 pint) chicken stock
1 clove of garlic, skinned and crushed
bayleaf
salt and pepper
grated cheese

Heat the butter and oil in the uncovered pressure cooker and lightly fry the onion until transparent and yellow. Stir in the mushrooms and cook for a few minutes, then remove from the cooker. Cut each chicken liver into four pieces and toss them in the seasoned flour. Fry livers gently in the remaining fat, stirring frequently, for about 5 minutes, until just firm and cooked. Remove livers from the cooker. Return the onions and mushrooms to the cooker with the rice, adding a little extra fat if required. Cook the rice, stirring well, until it has browned. Stir in the stock, garlic, bayleaf and seasoning. Bring to the boil, stirring well. Put on the lid and bring to high (15 lb) pressure. Cook for 7 minutes. Reduce pressure quickly. Add the chicken livers to the risotto and continue to cook gently over low heat for about 2 minutes, to reheat the livers. Remove the bayleaf. Pile the risotto on to a hot dish and serve with grated cheese.

Prawn risotto

25 g (1 oz) butter
30 ml (2 tbsp) oil
1 medium-size onion, skinned and chopped
50 g (2 oz) mushrooms, chopped
225 g (8 oz) long grain rice
600 ml (1 pint) chicken stock
bayleaf
1 clove of garlic, skinned and crushed
30 ml (2 level tbsp) tomato paste
salt and pepper
200 g (7 oz) peeled prawns
grated cheese

Heat the butter and oil in the uncovered pressure

Prawn risotto

pressure. Cook for 5 minutes. Reduce pressure slowly. Fluff the rice with a fork. Rinse and dry the cooker and pour in the oil. Lightly fry the onions in the uncovered cooker until they are golden brown, then stir in the ham and cook for about 1 minute. Lastly stir in the rice and cook it for about 2–3 minutes. Add pepper and parsley, adjust the seasoning and serve in a hot dish with grated cheese handed separately.

Savoury brown rice

This rice has whole unpolished grains with only the inedible husk and a small amount of bran removed. It requires longer cooking than white rice and has a chewy, nutty texture when cooked. It makes a pleasant variation from long grain rice.

1 medium-size onion, skinned and chopped
1 celery stalk, washed, trimmed and chopped
50 g (2 oz) butter or margarine
1 clove of garlic, skinned and crushed
225 g (8 oz) brown rice
salt and pepper
450 ml (¾ pint) chicken stock
50 g (2 oz) raisins
50 g (2 oz) flaked brown almonds

Fry the onion and celery in the fat in the uncovered pressure cooker until it is just brown. Stir in the crushed garlic and rice; cook, stirring, for about 3 minutes. Sprinkle with salt and pepper and pour on the stock. Bring to the boil and stir well. Put on the lid and slowly bring to high (15 lb) pressure. Cook for 15 minutes. Reduce pressure quickly. Stir in the raisins and almonds. If all the liquid has not been absorbed, cook over gentle heat in the uncovered cooker until the rice is dry, stirring it with a fork now and again. Serve with grated cheese or as an accompaniment to meat or vegetable dishes.

cooker and fry the onion and mushrooms until lightly brown. Stir in the rice and continue to cook until the rice has browned. Remove cooker from the heat and stir in the stock, bayleaf, garlic, tomato paste and seasoning. Bring to the boil and stir well to ensure that no rice grains are stuck to the base of the pan. Put on the lid and bring to high (15 lb) pressure. Cook for 7 minutes. Reduce the pressure quickly. Stir the risotto well with a fork and add the prawns. If all the cooking liquid has not been absorbed, stir over gentle heat until the rice is dry and the grains are separated. Adjust the seasoning and remove the bayleaf. Serve with grated cheese.

Fried rice with ham

225 g (8 oz) long grain rice
5 ml (1 level tsp) salt
600 ml (1 pint) chicken stock
45 ml (3 tbsp) oil
2 medium-size onions, skinned and sliced
100 g (4 oz) cooked ham, diced
freshly ground pepper
15 ml (1 tbsp) chopped parsley
Parmesan or Cheddar cheese

Put 300 ml (½ pint) water in the pressure cooker with the trivet. Put the rice, sprinkled with salt, in a solid container or ovenproof dish. Pour on the stock and stand the container on the trivet. Cover with foil. Put on the lid and bring to high (15 lb)

General instructions for cooking pasta in the pressure cooker

There are many varieties of pasta, but most of them are made from the same basic dough (with or without egg). They differ only in shape and size and the cooking times vary accordingly.

The cooking guide given below does not include every available pasta, but experience will help when calculating the pressure cooking times of those not mentioned. All the times given below refer to dried pasta and not freshly made pasta, which requires only about 5 minutes normal cooking.

Cook the pasta according to the recipe or follow the instructions below:

1. Allow about 50–75 g (2–3 oz) pasta per head.

2. Put at least 1·7 litres (3 pints) water and 15 ml (1 level tbsp) salt into the pressure cooker, without the trivet, and bring to the boil.

3. Put in the pasta, gently lowering the long varieties until completely immersed. (Never have the cooker more than half full.) Stir well for a good minute to prevent the pasta sticking to the base. Gently bring to the boil.

4. Put on the lid, lower the heat and slowly bring to high (15 lb) pressure, keeping the heat a little lower than usual.

5. Cook according to the time shown in the cooking guide, taking care that the pasta does not froth up and spurt through the vent. If this should happen, remove the cooker from the heat and shake the pan gently to allow the pasta to subside. Wipe round the vent and continue cooking gently.

6. Reduce pressure quickly and strain the pasta through a colander.

7. Put 25 g (1 oz) butter and 15 ml (1 tbsp) oil in the cooker and toss the pasta in it before putting it in a hot dish.

8. Wash the cooker thoroughly, especially round the gasket and vent on the lid to ensure they are not blocked.

Most pastas can be served with a variety of sauces. Recipes for several sauces are given and they can be used with any pasta. Spaghetti, for example, does not necessarily have to be served with Bolognese sauce.

When cooking a complete pasta meal in a pressure cooker, it is advisable to make the sauce first and keep it hot while the pasta is cooking. Some sauces, such as Bolognese or mariner's, are improved in texture if allowed to simmer gently for

Guide to pressure cooking pasta

	Cooking time at high (15 lb) pressure
Macaroni – elbow	5–6 minutes
5 cm (2 in) lengths	4–5 minutes
Spaghetti	3–4 minutes
Cannelloni	7 minutes
Tagliatelle	3–4 minutes
Vermicelli	3 minutes
Shells	3–4 minutes
Noodles	3 minutes

about 5 minutes over low heat after reducing pressure.

Bolognese sauce

This quantity is sufficient for 225 g (8 oz) pasta.

50 g (2 oz) green bacon, rinded and chopped
25 g (1 oz) butter or margarine
1 small onion, skinned and chopped
1 carrot, pared and finely chopped
1 stick of celery, washed, trimmed and chopped
225 g (8 oz) finely minced beef
1 clove of garlic, skinned and crushed
100 g (4 oz) chicken livers, finely chopped
30 ml (2 level tbsp) tomato paste
150 ml (¼ pint) dry white wine
150 ml (¼ pint) stock
salt and pepper
nutmeg
bayleaf

Fry the bacon in the butter or margarine in the uncovered pressure cooker until it is just brown. Then add the vegetables and fry for a further 5 minutes until brown. Stir in the beef and garlic and mix well to break up the lumps in the meat. Then add the chopped livers and continue frying for about 3 minutes. Add the tomato paste, wine, stock, seasoning, nutmeg and bayleaf and mix well. Put on the lid and bring to high (15 lb) pressure. Cook for 5 minutes. Reduce pressure quickly. Remove the bayleaf and adjust seasoning. Put in a hot dish and keep hot while the pasta is cooking, or let it simmer gently in a pan for about 5 minutes.

Beef curry (see page 72) ▶

Milanese sauce

This quantity is sufficient for 225 g (8 oz) pasta.

1 small onion, skinned and chopped
50 g (2 oz) mushrooms, chopped
25 g (1 oz) butter
425-g (15-oz) can of tomatoes
1 clove of garlic, skinned and crushed
150 ml (¼ pint) stock
bayleaf
pinch of dried thyme
pinch of dried oregano or marjoram
5 ml (1 level tsp) sugar
salt and pepper
50 g (2 oz) ham, chopped
50 g (2 oz) tongue, chopped

Fry the onion and mushrooms in the melted butter in the uncovered pressure cooker for 2–3 minutes. Stir in the tomatoes with the juice, the garlic, stock, herbs, sugar and seasonings. Put on the lid and bring to high (15 lb) pressure. Cook for 5 minutes. Reduce pressure quickly. Add the ham and tongue, adjust the seasoning and remove the bayleaf. Reheat for 2–3 minutes, then serve with the cooked pasta. If the sauce is too runny, boil it rapidly in the uncovered cooker for a few minutes to reduce it a little.

Mariner's sauce

This quantity is sufficient for 225 g (8 oz) pasta.

50 g (2 oz) streaky bacon rashers, rinded and
    chopped
2 medium-size onions, skinned and finely chopped
2 sticks of celery, washed, trimmed and finely
    chopped
30 ml (2 tbsp) oil
450 g (1 lb) tomatoes, skinned and chopped or 425-g
    (15-oz) can of tomatoes, chopped
30 ml (2 level tbsp) tomato paste
150 ml (¼ pint) stock
1 large clove of garlic, skinned and crushed
bouquet garni
pepper
pinch of sugar
60-g (2-oz) can of anchovies, drained and chopped

Fry the bacon, onions and celery in the heated oil in the uncovered pressure cooker until just lightly browned. Stir in the tomatoes with the juice, paste, stock, garlic, bouquet garni, pepper and

sugar. Put on the lid and bring to high (15 lb) pressure. Cook for 5 minutes. Reduce pressure quickly. Stir in the anchovies, reheat for about one minute.

Fresh tomato sauce

This quantity is sufficient for 225 g (8 oz) pasta.

1 large onion, skinned and chopped
25 g (1 oz) butter
15 ml (1 tbsp) oil
700 g (1½ lb) tomatoes, skinned and quartered
30 ml (2 level tbsp) tomato paste
1 clove of garlic, skinned and crushed
bayleaf
2·5 ml (½ level tsp) dried oregano or marjoram
salt
freshly ground pepper
150 ml (¼ pint) chicken stock

Lightly fry the onion in the butter and oil in the uncovered pressure cooker. Stir in the tomatoes and cook for 2–3 minutes. Add the tomato paste, garlic, bayleaf, oregano and seasoning. Pour in the stock, put on the lid and bring to high (15 lb) pressure. Cook for 5 minutes. Reduce pressure quickly. Remove the bayleaf. Sieve the sauce or purée it in an electric blender, then return it to the cooker; reheat, uncovered, and reduce slightly so that it has a thick creamy consistency.

Chicken liver sauce

This quantity is sufficient for 225 g (8 oz) pasta.

1 large onion, skinned and chopped
25 g (1 oz) butter
100 g (4 oz) mushrooms, chopped
225 g (8 oz) chicken livers
30 ml (2 level tbsp) seasoned flour
300 ml (½ pint) chicken stock
1 clove of garlic, skinned and crushed
bouquet garni
15 ml (1 level tbsp) tomato paste
salt
freshly ground pepper
30 ml (2 tbsp) dry sherry

Fry the onion very lightly in the melted butter in the uncovered cooker, then fry the mushrooms. Toss the livers in the seasoned flour, add them to the cooker and fry lightly until just firm. Add the stock, garlic, bouquet garni, tomato paste and seasoning. Put on the lid and bring to high (15 lb) pressure. Cook for 5 minutes. Reduce pressure quickly. Remove the bouquet garni. Blend the sauce into a smooth consistency with a fork or in an electric blender, but do not make it too smooth. Add the sherry and adjust the seasoning. Reheat in the uncovered cooker.

Tomato macaroni cheese

40 g (1 ½ oz) butter or margarine
60 ml (4 level tbsp) flour
586 ml (1 pint) milk
175 g (6 oz) mature cheese, grated
salt and pepper
2·5 ml (½ level tsp) dry mustard
175 g (6 oz) short cut macaroni
3 medium-size tomatoes, skinned
6 small bacon rashers, made into rolls (see below)

Melt the butter in a small pan, stir in the flour and cook for 2–3 minutes. Remove the pan from the heat and gradually stir in the milk. Bring to the boil and continue to stir until the sauce thickens. Then stir in three quarters of the cheese and the seasonings.

Meanwhile cook the macaroni for 4–5 minutes (see page 80) at high (15 lb) pressure in the cooker. Reduce pressure quickly. Strain the macaroni. Stir the macaroni into the cheese sauce and put in an ovenproof dish. Slice the tomatoes and arrange them round the edge of the macaroni cheese, sprinkle with seasoning and put the remaining grated cheese in the centre, sprinkling a little over the tomatoes. Brown under a hot grill and garnish with the bacon rolls. Serve with triangles of toast and green salad.

Bacon rolls
Cut the rind off the bacon and stretch each rasher with the back of a knife until it is very thin. Cut each rasher in half and roll it up. Secure the roll with a skewer and grill until crisp and brown.

Vermicelli savoury

In place of prawns, shrimps or canned flaked tuna, salmon or mackerel may be used.

100 g (4 oz) vermicelli
50 g (2 oz) butter
1 medium-size onion, skinned and chopped
15 ml (1 level tbsp) curry powder
150 g (6 oz) fresh, or frozen and thawed, peeled prawns
30 ml (2 level tbsp) mayonnaise
5 ml (1 level tsp) tomato paste
30 ml (2 tbsp) double cream, optional
5 ml (1 tsp) lemon juice
salt
freshly ground pepper
100 g (4 oz) finely grated mature cheese

Cook the vermicelli in the pressure cooker at high (15 lb) pressure for 3 minutes (see page 80). Drain pasta well and return it to the cooker with 25 g (1 oz) butter, toss well, then put the vermicelli in a hot ovenproof dish and keep it hot.

Meanwhile lightly fry the onion in the rest of the butter until just tender, then fry the curry powder for about 2 minutes. Remove the pan from the heat and stir in the prawns, until they are well covered with the spices. Stir in the mayonnaise, tomato paste, cream, lemon juice and seasoning. Mix well and spoon the mixture into the centre of the vermicelli. Sprinkle with the cheese and brown under a hot grill. Serve with cucumber and yoghurt salad.

Sausage balls with noodles

350 g (12 oz) sausagemeat
seasoned flour
15 ml (1 tbsp) oil
2 medium-size onions, skinned and chopped
425-g (15-oz) can of tomatoes
30 ml (2 level tbsp) tomato paste
150 ml (¼ pint) stock
1 clove of garlic, skinned and crushed
bouquet garni
5 ml (1 level tsp) sugar
salt
freshly ground pepper
225 g (8 oz) egg noodles
25–50 g (1–2 oz) butter
grated cheese

Divide the sausage meat into twelve small balls and roll them in a little seasoned flour. Fry gently in the oil in the uncovered pressure cooker until just brown. Remove the meat and fry the onions until just transparent, then stir in the tomatoes and their juice, tomato paste, stock, garlic, bouquet garni, sugar and seasoning. Put back the meat balls. Put on the lid and bring to high (15 lb) pressure. Cook for 5 minutes. Reduce pressure quickly. Remove the bouquet garni and spoon the contents of the cooker into a hot dish.

Meanwhile cook the noodles in the pressure cooker at high (15 lb) pressure for 3 minutes (see page 80). Reduce pressure quickly. Strain the noodles and put them in a separate hot dish with a knob of butter. Serve with grated cheese.

Breakfast porridge

600 ml (1 pint) water
120 ml (8 level tbsp) coarse oatmeal
5 ml (1 level tsp) salt
cream
sugar or salt, for serving

Put the water in the pressure cooker without the trivet and bring to the boil. Stir in the oatmeal and salt and bring to the boil again, uncovered, stir well and lower the heat. Put on the lid and gently bring to high (15 lb) pressure. Cook for 30 minutes, keeping the heat slightly lower than usual. (If the porridge froths up and through the vent, remove the cooker from the heat and wipe around the top carefully, then continue to cook.) Reduce pressure slowly. Serve porridge with cream and sugar or salt as desired. If the porridge is too thick, dilute it with a little boiling water; if it is too thin, stir it in the uncovered pan over gentle heat until the right consistency is reached.

FRUIT AND DESSERTS

A variety of cold sweets and desserts can, with either a fruit or custard base, be prepared and quickly cooked in a pressure cooker. Such dishes are useful for entertaining or summer cooking as they can be cooked well ahead of the meal and served cold.

Fruits vary so much in size, composition and texture that it is difficult to give hard and fast rules about cooking them in a pressure cooker. As a general rule it is advisable to pressure cook only the hard or stoned fruits, which normally take longer cooking. Unless a purée is required, it is best not to pressure cook soft fruits.

Dried fruits, which normally require long soaking and cooking, are excellent pressure cooked as they need only about a quarter of the normal cooking time and have a rich, mature flavour when cooked in this way (see page 91).

Some fruits are best cooked with sugar in an ovenproof container or solid separator, others can be cooked in the cooker (without the trivet) in a sugar syrup (see page 125) or fruit juice. As with all pressure cooking, never use less than 150–300 ml (¼–½ pint) liquid (according to type or manufacturer's instructions). The chart on pages 89–91 is a guide to cooking fruit in a pressure cooker, but freshness and age of fruit are really the deciding factors on the length of time required.

Milk puddings and custards are also excellent when cooked in a pressure cooker. Far less than normal cooking time is required, and when the instructions are precisely followed very good results are achieved.

Chocolate pears

100 g (4 oz) sugar
300 ml (½ pint) water
four underripe dessert pears – about 450 g (1 lb) in
**   total weight**
100 g (4 oz) plain cooking chocolate, broken into
**   pieces**
150 ml (¼ pint) milk
angelica cut into leaf shapes
whipped cream

Dissolve the sugar in the water in a saucepan over very low heat. Meanwhile, peel, halve and core the pears. When the sugar is completely dissolved, boil it for 2–3 minutes. Put the pears in a solid separator or ovenproof dish and cover with the sugar syrup. Put the trivet in the pressure cooker and pour in 300 ml (½ pint) water. Place the container of pears on the trivet. Put on the lid and bring to high (15 lb) pressure. Cook the pears for 7 minutes. Reduce the pressure quickly. Test for tenderness. Carefully lift out the pears and leave to drain and cool. Keep the syrup to use with other fruit.

Put the chocolate in a bowl with the milk and heat it over a saucepan of hot water until melted, stirring to mix it; leave to cool slightly. Arrange the pears on a flat serving dish and when the chocolate sauce is at coating consistency, spoon it over the pears and leave to set. Decorate with angelica and cream.

Prune mould

225 g (8 oz) prunes
300 ml (½ pint) water
50 g (2 oz) soft brown sugar
2–3 pieces lemon rind
45 ml (3 tbsp) sherry
15 ml (3 level tsp) powdered gelatine
142-ml (¼-pint) carton of whipping cream

Pour enough boiling water over the prunes to cover and soak for at least 30 minutes. Drain off

Prune mould

soaking water. Put prunes into the pressure cooker with the measured water, sugar and lemon rind. Put on the lid and bring to high (15 lb) pressure. Cook for 13 minutes. Reduce pressure quickly. Leave the prunes to cool. Remove the prune stones (reserving a few) and lemon rind and sieve the fruit or purée it in an electric blender. There should be just over 450 ml (¾ pint) of fruit purée.

Crack a few prune stones and remove the kernels; blanch them in boiling water and remove the skin. Add the kernels to the purée. Put the sherry in a small basin and sprinkle over the gelatine, then warm it over a little hot water until the gelatine has dissolved. Whip the cream. Stir the gelatine into the prune purée and, when this is on the point of setting, fold in the whipped cream. Mix well and pour the mixture into a 600-ml (1-pint) mould; leave to set. When firm, turn the mould on to a dish and serve with extra cream and sponge fingers.

Apricot fool

Apricot condé

225 g (8 oz) fresh apricots, halved and stoned
25 g (1 oz) sugar
150 ml (¼ pint) water
30 ml (2 tbsp) water
15 ml (3 level tsp) powdered gelatine
113-g (4-oz) carton of whipping cream
30 ml (2 level tbsp) redcurrant jelly
15 ml (1 level tbsp) arrowroot

For the creamy rice

25 g (1 oz) butter
568 ml (1 pint) milk
50 g (2 oz) pudding rice
50 g (2 oz) sugar

Make the rice as for Creamy rice pudding (see page 86) but do not brown under grill. Leave it to get quite cold, stirring now and again. Put the apricots, sugar and water in a solid separator or ovenproof dish. Put the trivet in the pressure cooker and pour in 300 ml (½ pint) water. Stand the separator containing the apricots on the trivet. Put on the lid and bring to high (15 lb) pressure. Cook for 3–4 minutes. Reduce pressure quickly. Remove the fruit and drain, reserving the liquid. Leave the apricots to cool.

Put the 30 ml (2 tbsp) water in a small basin and sprinkle over the gelatine. Warm it gently over hot water until dissolved; leave until cool and almost on the point of setting. Whip the cream. Stir the gelatine into the cold creamed rice, mix well, then fold in the whipped cream. Pour the mixture into a glass dish and leave to set. Arrange the halved apricots over the top. Heat the apricot liquid in a small pan with the redcurrant jelly until it is almost at boiling point. Blend the arrowroot to a paste with a little water, then stir in a little of the hot liquid. Add the mixture to the pan, stirring until it boils. Leave the sauce to cool, then spoon a little over the apricots. Serve the remaining sauce separately.

Apricot fool

225 g (8 oz) dried apricots
75 g (3 oz) sugar
300 ml (½ pint) water
10 ml (2 level tsp) grated orange rind
30 ml (2 tbsp) orange juice
142-ml (¼-pint) carton of whipping cream
twists of orange peel
angelica cut into leaf shapes

Pour enough boiling water over the apricots to

cover and soak for at least 30 minutes. Put the drained apricots in the pressure cooker with the sugar, measured water, orange rind and juice. Put on the lid and bring to high (15 lb) pressure. Cook for 10 minutes. Reduce pressure quickly. Sieve the apricots or purée them in an electric blender. Leave to get quite cold. Whip the cream, fold it into the cold purée and mix well. Divide the fool into 4–6 individual glasses and decorate each with a twist of orange peel and angelica.

SERVES 4–6

Blackberry and apple snow

450 g (1 lb) cooking apples, peeled and cored
100 g (4 oz) sugar
225 g (8 oz) blackberries, washed and picked over
2 egg whites
4–6 blackberries for decoration

Put the sliced apples in a solid separator or ovenproof dish with 50 g (2 oz) sugar. Put the blackberries in another container and sprinkle with the rest of the sugar. Pour 300 ml (½ pint) water into the pressure cooker, put in the trivet and the two fruits. Put on the lid and bring to high (15 lb) pressure. Cook for 5–6 minutes. Reduce pressure slowly. Using a fork or whisk, beat the apples until quite smooth. Sieve the blackberries and discard the seeds. Mix the two fruits together and leave to get quite cold. Whisk the egg whites to soft peak consistency and fold them into the apple mixture. Spoon into 4–6 individual glasses and top each with a whole blackberry.

SERVES 4–6

Brandied cherries

450 g (1 lb) black or morello cherries, pricked
100 g (4 oz) sugar
pinch of ground cinnamon
300 ml (½ pint) water
15 ml (1 level tbsp) arrowroot
60 ml (4 tbsp) brandy

Prick the cherries with a needle or fine skewer to prevent them bursting. Put them with the sugar, cinnamon and water into the pressure cooker. Put on the lid and bring to high (15 lb) pressure. Cook

for 5 minutes. Reduce pressure quickly. Using a draining spoon, transfer the cherries to a dish. Blend the arrowroot to a smooth paste with 30 ml (2 tbsp) cold water, stir in a little of the hot fruit juice, then add the mixture to the cooker; bring to the boil, stirring as the sauce thickens. Remove the cooker from heat and stir in the brandy. Pour the sauce over the cherries and leave, covered, until cold. Serve with ice cream or creamed rice.

Blackcurrant mallow

450 g (1 lb) blackcurrants, washed
175 g (6 oz) sugar
300 ml (½ pint) water
25 ml (5 level tsp) powdered gelatine
1 egg white
10 marshmallows

Put the blackcurrants, sugar and water into the pressure cooker. Put on the lid and bring to high (15 lb) pressure. Cook for 4–5 minutes. Reduce pressure slowly. Sieve the blackcurrants or purée them in an electric blender. (If an electric blender is used, the blackcurrants should be sieved afterwards to remove the seeds.) Leave to cool.

Put 60 ml (4 tbsp) water in a small basin and sprinkle the gelatine over. Heat gently over a pan of hot water until dissolved. Then stir the gelatine into the blackcurrant purée and leave until it is almost on the point of setting. Whisk the egg white to stiff peak stage. Cut the marshmallows into quarters with a wetted knife and add them to the egg whites. Gradually fold in the blackcurrant purée and, when well mixed, pour into a glass dish. Serve with cream and shortbread biscuits.

Creamy rice pudding

25 g (1 oz) butter
just under 568 ml (1 pint) milk
50 g (2 oz) pudding rice
50 g (2 oz) sugar
grated nutmeg

Melt the butter in the uncovered pressure cooker. Pour in the milk and bring to the boil. Stir in the rice and sugar. Stir well, bring to the boil again, then lower the heat until the mixture just simmers. Put on the lid and slowly bring to high (15 lb) pressure. Cook for 5 minutes. Reduce pressure slowly. Stir the rice and put it into an ovenproof dish. Sprinkle with nutmeg and brown under a hot grill.

Crème brûlée

568 ml (1 pint) whipping cream
vanilla pod or 5 ml (1 tsp) vanilla essence
4 egg yolks
75 ml (5 level tbsp) caster sugar

Heat the cream and vanilla in a small pan to just below scalding point. Whisk the egg yolks and 15 ml (1 level tbsp) caster sugar together until creamy and light in colour. Remove the vanilla pod, if using, and whisk the cream into the egg mixture. Pour into a greased soufflé dish to give a depth of about 4 cm (1 ½ in) and cover with foil. Put 300 ml (½ pint) water in the pressure cooker, put in the trivet and stand the custard on it. Bring to high (15 lb) pressure. Cook for 5 minutes. Reduce pressure slowly. Take out the dish, let it cool, then chill it.

Just before the pudding is required, put a collar of foil round the edge of the dish to prevent it cracking. Heat the grill until it is really glowing hot. Sprinkle the custard with a thick layer of caster sugar and place it under the grill. When the sugar has melted and browned, remove it and take off the foil. Chill again before serving.

Bread and butter pudding

50 g (2 oz) very thin slices of bread, buttered
30 ml (2 level tbsp) marmalade
50 g (2 oz) sultanas
2 eggs
25 g (1 oz) caster sugar
300 ml (½ pint) milk
2·5 ml (½ level tsp) mixed spice
30 ml (2 level tbsp) demerara sugar
few shavings of butter

Spread the buttered bread with the marmalade and cut it into fingers or quarters. Arrange the bread in layers in a greased 600-ml (1-pint) ovenproof dish with the sultanas sprinkled between the layers. Whisk together the eggs and sugar until light and creamy. Heat the milk almost

Bread and butter pudding

to boiling point and pour it into the egg mixture; mix well, then pour the custard on to the bread and butter. Leave to soak for about 10 minutes.

Pour 300 ml (½ pint) water in the pressure cooker and put in the trivet. Sprinkle the spice over the pudding, cover with foil and place the dish on the trivet. Put on the lid and bring to high (15 lb) pressure. Cook for 6 minutes. Reduce pressure slowly. Sprinkle the top with the demerara sugar and dot with butter, then put under a hot grill to brown.

Apricot caramel cream

See colour picture facing page 81

60 ml (4 tbsp) apricot jam
3 eggs
25 g (1 oz) caster sugar
400 ml (¾ pint) milk
100 g (4 oz) granulated sugar
150 ml (¼ pint) water
150 ml (¼ pint) whipping cream

Butter a deep 15-cm (6-in) soufflé dish and put the jam in the base. Whisk the eggs and caster sugar together until light and creamy in colour. Heat the milk almost to boiling and whisk it into the egg mixture. Pour the mixture gently into the prepared dish and cover with foil. Pour 300 ml (½ pint) water in the pressure cooker and put in the trivet. Stand the custard on the trivet and put on the lid of the cooker. Bring to high (15 lb) pressure and cook for 5 minutes. Reduce pressure slowly. Remove the custard from the cooker and leave it to get cold.

Meanwhile put the granulated sugar and water in a small heavy based pan and place it on gentle heat. When the sugar is completely dissolved, increase the heat and boil until the syrup is golden. Pour the syrup on to an oiled baking sheet and leave it until cold. Whip the cream until it is stiff and spread half of it over the cold custard. Pipe the remaining cream to form a border round the edge. Crush the caramel with a rolling pin and spoon it into the centre of the dish. Serve chilled.

Gooseberry crunchy pudding

Rhubarb, apples, or plums may be used in place of gooseberries; cook as described on pages 89–91.

450 g (1 lb) gooseberries, topped and tailed
50 g (2 oz) sugar
75 g (3 oz) butter
100 g (4 oz) fresh breadcrumbs
100 g (4 oz) demerara sugar

Place gooseberries in solid container, sprinkle with the sugar and cover with foil. Put 300 ml (½ pint) water in the pressure cooker with the trivet and stand the gooseberries on the trivet. Put on the lid and bring to high (15 lb) pressure. Cook for 4 minutes. Reduce pressure slowly. Strain the gooseberries so that only the fruit is used.

Melt 50 g (2 oz) butter in a frying pan and fry the breadcrumbs until golden. Remove the crumbs from the pan and mix with half the demerara sugar. Grease a 600-ml (1-pint) ovenproof soufflé dish or small casserole that will fit in the cooker and put a layer of gooseberries on the bottom, then sprinkle with a layer of the crumb mixture. Build up in layers, finishing with a crumb layer. Cover the dish with greased foil, tie round the rim with string and make a handle. Put 600 ml (1 pint) water into the pressure cooker, put in the trivet and stand the pudding in the cooker. Bring to high (15 lb)

pressure. Cook for 10 minutes. Reduce pressure slowly. Take out the pudding and remove the foil. Dot the pudding with the remaining butter and sprinkle with the rest of the sugar, then brown it under a hot grill.

Rich chocolate cream

4 large macaroon biscuits
100 g (4 oz) plain cooking chocolate, broken into pieces
400 ml (¾ pint) single cream
3 eggs
50 g (2 oz) caster sugar
6–8 small ratafia biscuits
whipped cream
grated chocolate or toasted flaked almonds

Crush the macaroon biscuits and put them in a greased 900-ml (1½-pint) soufflé dish. Heat the cooking chocolate and cream in a saucepan almost to boiling point. Whisk the eggs and sugar in a bowl until light and creamy. Then pour on the chocolate mixture. Mix well, then gently pour the mixture into the soufflé dish. Leave to stand for about 5 minutes, then cover with foil.

Put 300 ml (½ pint) water into the pressure cooker with the trivet and stand the chocolate custard on the trivet. Put on the lid and bring to high (15 lb) pressure. Cook for 10 minutes. Reduce pressure slowly. Leave the chocolate custard to cool, then chill it. Arrange the ratafia biscuits on top and decorate with a little whipped cream and grated chocolate or toasted almonds.

Vienna pudding

25 g (1 oz) granulated sugar
30 ml (2 tbsp) water
300 ml (½ pint) milk
100 g (4 oz) trifle sponge cakes
25 g (1 oz) sultanas
25 g (1 oz) glacé cherries, cut into quarters
45 ml (3 tbsp) sherry
2 eggs
25 g (1 oz) caster sugar
sweetened gooseberry or apricot purée (see pages 91, 90)

Put the granulated sugar into a small saucepan and heat with water over very low heat until the sugar dissolves. Then increase the heat and cook until the sugar turns to a dark golden brown. Remove the pan from the heat and carefully pour in the milk (this will splutter) and reheat gently to dissolve the caramel. Cut the sponge cakes into 2·5-cm (1-in) pieces, mix with the sultanas and cherries and put into a greased 600-ml (1-pint) ovenproof dish or mould. Pour on the sherry and leave to soak.

Whisk together the eggs and caster sugar until light and creamy, then whisk in the caramel milk. Pour the mixture on to the sponge cakes and leave to soak for about 10 minutes, then cover with foil. Put 300 ml (½ pint) water in the pressure cooker and put in the trivet. Stand the pudding on the trivet and put on the lid. Bring to high (15 lb) pressure. Cook for 15 minutes. Reduce pressure slowly. Serve with a gooseberry or apricot purée.

Cooking guide to pressure cooking fruit

Soft fruits should be covered with foil and the pressure should be reduced slowly to prevent the fruit spluttering. Do the same if cooking fruit for a purée in a container.

Fruit	Preparation	Pressure cooking at high (15 lb) pressure	Serving suggestions
Apples	*Whole* Core and cut round the skin at the widest part. Put in an ovenproof dish or solid separator.	4–6 minutes, depending on size and stuffing.	Serve with whipped cream or custard.
	Sliced or quartered Put in a heatproof dish or solid separator, sprinkle with sugar or add 30–45 ml (2–3 tbsp) sugar syrup.	4–5 minutes, depending on thickness of the dish.	Serve with whipped cream or custard.
	Puréed Peel, core and slice apples and put in cooker without trivet; add at least 150 ml (¼ pint) water. Sieve or purée in an electric blender when cooked.	5 minutes. Reduce pressure slowly.	Use for making fruit creams, apple sauce and other cold sweets.
Apricots	*Halved* Wash and cut in halves. Remove stones and put them a bag or muslin to add flavour. Put fruit into ovenproof dish or solid separator, sprinkle with sugar or 30–45 ml (2–3 tbsp) sugar syrup (see page 125).	4–5 minutes depending upon maturity of the fruit.	Serve with whipped cream or custard. Use for decorating other cold sweets.

Fruit	Preparation	Pressure cooking at high (15 lb) pressure	Serving suggestions
	Purée Wash, halve and remove stones. Put in 150 ml (¼ pint) sugar syrup (see page 125) in cooker without trivet Sieve or purée in an electric blender when cooked.	4–5 minutes	For sauces, fruit creams and ice cream.
Blackberries	*Whole* Wash and pick over. Put into an ovenproof dish or solid separator, sprinkle with sugar or add 30–45 ml (2–3 tbsp) sugar syrup (see page 125). Cover with foil.	5 minutes. Reduce pressure slowly.	With apple quarters or other fruits; with whipped cream or custard.
	Purée Wash and pick over. Put into cooker, without trivet, with at least 150 ml (¼ pint) sugar syrup (see page 125). Sieve or purée in an electric blender when cooked.	5–6 minutes	For fruit creams, sauces and ice cream.
Blackcurrants and other currants	String and wash. Put into an ovenproof dish or solid separator, sprinkle with sugar or 30–45 ml (2–3 tbsp) sugar syrup (see page 125). Cover with foil.	4–5 minutes. Reduce pressure slowly.	With whipped cream custard; in summer pudding.
	Purée Wash and put into pressure cooker, without trivet, with at least 150 ml (¼ pint) sugar syrup (see page 125). Sieve or purée in an electric blender when cooked.	5–6 minutes. Reduce pressure slowly.	For fruit creams, sauces and ice cream or water ice.
Cherries, morello, black or white	Wash and put into oven-proof dish or container, without trivet, with at least 150 ml (¼ pint) sugar syrup (see page 125).	4 minutes	For fruit pies, filling, or cold sweets; with whipped cream or custard.
Gooseberries	*Whole* Top and tail, put into an ovenproof dish or solid separator, sprinkle with sugar or add 30–45 ml (2–3 tbsp) sugar syrup (see page 125). Cover with foil.	4 minutes. Reduce pressure slowly.	For pies, and fruit fillings for flans; with cream or custard.

Fruit	Preparation	Pressure cooking at high (15 lb) pressure	Serving suggestions
	Purée Put into cooker with not less than 150 ml (¼ pint) sugar syrup (page 125) or water. Sieve or purée in electric blender when cooked.	5 minutes. Reduce pressure slowly.	For sauces, fools and other cold sweets.
Pears, underripe dessert	*Halved* Peel, halve and core. Put into ovenproof dish or solid separator with sugar syrup (see page 125) to cover.	7–8 minutes	With cream, custard or ice cream; with other fruit or chocolate sauce.
Pears, hard cooking	Peel, halve and core. Put into ovenproof dish or solid separator with sugar syrup (see page 125) to cover.	12–15 minutes, depending upon variety.	As above.
Plums and other stone fruits	Wash and stalk. Halve and remove stones if wished. Put into ovenproof dish or solid container with sugar syrup (see page 125) to cover.	4–5 minutes (less if halved)	For pies and fruit flan fillings, or serve with cream or custard.
Rhubarb	Wash and cut into 3-cm (1¼-in) lengths. Put in ovenproof dish or other container, sprinkle with sugar. Cover with foil.	Garden, 2 minutes. Reduce pressure slowly.	For pies, fruit flans, fools and other cold sweets.

Guide to pressure cooking dried fruit

Pour 600 ml (1 pint) boiling water over 225 g (8 oz) fruit and leave to soak at least 30 minutes before cooking. Drain off the remaining soaking water. Put fruit in the pressure cooker without the trivet and add 300 ml (½ pint) water. Add about 50 g (2 oz) sugar or sugar syrup (see page 125), according to taste, and flavouring, if wished (see below). Cook for the time shown in the chart, according to type of fruit.

Fruit	Pressure cooking at high (15 lb) pressure	Suggested flavourings
Apple rings	5–6 minutes	1–2 cloves, little lemon peel and juice, blackberry syrup.
Dried apricots	Whole, 8 minutes Purée, 10 minutes	2–3 strips lemon or orange peel and lemon or orange juice.
Figs	8 minutes	2–3 strips lemon peel, 2·5-cm (1-in) piece of cinnamon stick.
Prunes	12 minutes	2–3 strips lemon peel; 2–3 drops almond essence; brown sugar instead of white for syrup
Mixed fruit salad	12 minutes	30–45 ml (2–3 tbsp) lemon juice and a few strips of lemon peel.

HEARTY PUDDINGS

Old fashioned suet and sponge puddings are inexpensive to make and are easily prepared. When cooked in a pressure cooker, they are even more economical as they can be made and served in less than one hour.

Most pudding recipes can be adapted for cooking in a pressure cooker. Christmas pudding can be cooked in far less time, and canned puddings may also be pressure cooked. As long as ovenproof watertight containers such as basins, moulds or foil bowls are used, and the instructions listed below are followed, excellent results should be obtained.

A pudding is first steamed in the cooker for a short time so that the raising agent can react in the heat and moisture and cause the pudding to rise. If the pudding were brought to pressure immediately, the pressure in the cooker would prevent it rising. This pre-steaming is done by putting on the lid without the weight and keeping the cooker over gentle heat so that the steam escapes through the open vent in a steady flow.

After the pre-steaming the cooker is brought to low (5 lb) pressure to ensure that the pudding is really light. Cookers which have fixed high (15 lb) pressure can be used only for cooking small individual portions in cups or dariole moulds, or for Christmas puddings, which need high pressure. The chart on page 99 gives steaming and cooking times.

Puddings are best left undisturbed during their cooking time, therefore it is advisable not to try to cook other foods in the pressure cooker at the same time. If the pressure cooker is needed for the rest of the meal, make and cook the pudding first, then keep it hot while using the pressure cooker again. Alternatively, cook the pudding in advance and reheat it while the rest of the meal is being served.

General instructions for making steamed puddings in the pressure cooker

1. Measure the correct amount of water in the pressure cooker. Do not use less than 1 litre (1¾ pints) water.

2. Put in the trivet and leave ready to heat to boiling point when required. A little vinegar added to the water will prevent discoloration of the aluminium cooker.

3. Choose a basin, mould or foil bowl that will fit easily into the cooker so that the steam can circulate easily around it. Grease the container and have ready a piece of greased foil or double thickness greaseproof paper to use to cover the pudding. Do not fill the basin more than three quarters (except for fruit suet puddings) so that the pudding has room to rise.

4. Prepare the pudding and put it in the greased container. Cover the pudding loosely with greased foil, or double greaseproof, allowing room for expansion, tie it in place round the basin rim with string and make a handle of string to go over the top. This will make it easier to lower the pudding into the boiling water in the cooker. If the container has no rim to support a handle, pass a strip of strong cotton or old ribbon under it and tie, and use this to lower the basin into the cooker.

5. Heat the water in the pressure cooker to boiling point, and put in the pudding, standing it on the trivet.

6. Put on the lid without the weight. Lower the heat and keep the water at simmering point so that there is a constant but gentle flow of steam escaping from the vent.

7. Steam for recommended time (see page 99).

8. Put on the weight and increase the heat to bring to low (5 lb) pressure, except in the case of small individual puddings or Christmas puddings which need high pressure. Cook for the required time (see page 99).

9. Reduce pressure slowly and remove pudding.

10. Take off the covering, loosen the pudding from the sides of the basin and turn it out on to a hot dish.

Canned ready made puddings may be reheated in the unopened can at low (5 lb) pressure. Allow 10 minutes for small cans, 20 minutes for large. Use at least 300 ml (½ pint) water in the cooker, more for a large can.

When increasing quantities given in the recipes, increase the pressure cooking time by 10 minutes to every additional 50 g (2 oz) flour. Increase the cooking water by 150 ml (¼ pint) to every additional 50 g (2 oz) flour. NB: Make sure the basin is not too large for easy circulation of steam.

To reheat a pudding from cold, put the pudding on the trivet in the pressure cooker containing about 600 ml (1 pint) boiling water. Put on the lid and bring to low (5 lb) pressure and reheat for about 10 minutes.

Rachel's delight

1·25 ml (¼ level tsp) bicarbonate of soda
15 ml (1 tbsp) milk
100 g (4 oz) flour
100 g (4 oz) fresh breadcrumbs
100 g (4 oz) shredded suet
25 g (1 oz) soft brown sugar
100 g (4 oz) raisins
90 ml (6 level tbsp) jam
150 ml (¼ pint) milk
pinch of salt

Grease a 900-ml (1½-pint) pudding basin. Dissolve the bicarbonate of soda in the tablespoon of milk and set aside. Put all the dry ingredients together in a bowl and mix to a soft dough with the jam and 150 ml (¼ pint) milk. Put 1 litre (1¾ pints) water in the pressure cooker and put in the trivet. Start boiling the water. Meanwhile, add the dissolved bicarbonate of soda to the pudding, mix well and put the mixture into the basin. Cover with greased foil, tie round rim with string and make a handle. Lower the pudding into the cooker. Put on the lid without the weight, lower the heat and steam for 15 minutes. Then increase the heat to bring to low (5 lb) pressure. Cook for 45 minutes. Reduce pressure slowly. Turn out pudding and serve with custard or brown butter hard sauce (see page 95).

Jam roly poly

Marmalade, mincemeat, chopped apples and dates, or syrup and breadcrumbs may be used in place of jam. A plain suet roll, without a filling, can be served with syrup, jam, honey or lemon curd.

225 g (8 oz) self raising flour
2·5 ml (½ level tsp) salt
100 g (4 oz) shredded suet
about 150 ml (¼ pint) cold water
90 ml (6 level tbsp) jam for filling

Make the suet crust pastry by mixing the dry ingredients to a soft dough with water. Knead the dough on a floured surface and roll it into a rectangle about 23 by 28 cm (9 by 11 in). Damp the edges with water. Spread the jam over the pastry to within 1 cm (½ in) of the sides. Starting from one of the narrow edges, roll the pastry making sure not to squeeze the jam out. Form it into a neat roll. Put the roll on a piece of greased foil and wrap it around loosely (to allow enough room for expansion) but seal the ends well.

Put 1 litre (1¾ pints) water in the pressure cooker and put in the trivet. Bring the water to the boil and put in the pudding. Put on the lid without the weight. Lower the heat and steam the pudding for 15 minutes. Put on the weight and increase the heat to bring to low (5 lb) pressure. Cook for 30 minutes. Reduce pressure slowly. Take out the pudding, remove the foil, and serve on a hot dish.

Treacle layer pudding

175–225 g (6–8 oz) golden syrup
50 g (2 oz) breadcrumbs
grated rind of 1 small lemon
extra syrup for serving, optional

For the suet crust pastry
225 g (8 oz) self raising flour
2·5 ml (½ level tsp) salt
100 g (4 oz) shredded suet
150 ml (¼ pint) cold water

To make the suet crust pastry, mix the dry ingredients to a soft dough with water and knead it on a floured surface. Divide the dough into 4–5 pieces each slightly larger than the previous one. Roll the pieces into rounds. Put the smallest layer on the bottom of a greased 900-ml (1½-pint) pudding basin. Mix together the syrup, breadcrumbs and lemon rind. Put a spoonful of filling on the first pastry round, then build up the pudding in layers, using a larger round each time and a spoonful of the filling between layers. Cover with greased foil, tie round rim with string and make a handle. Put 1 litre (1¾ pints) water in the pressure cooker, put in the trivet and bring to the boil. Lower pudding into the cooker. Put on the lid without the weight, then lower the heat and steam the pudding for 15 minutes. Then put on the weight and increase the heat to bring to low (5 lb) pressure. Cook for 45 minutes. Reduce pressure slowly. Remove the pudding from cooker and turn it out on to a hot dish. Serve with extra syrup if required.

Pineapple upside-down pudding

30 ml (2 level tbsp) golden syrup
340-g (12-oz) can of pineapple rings
15 ml (1 tbsp) lemon juice
25 g (1 oz) glacé cherries
75 g (3 oz) butter or block margarine
75 g (3 oz) caster sugar
1 egg
100 g (4 oz) self raising flour
grated rind of 1 small lemon
30 ml (2 tbsp) milk
15 ml (1 level tsp) arrowroot

Grease a 900-ml (1½-pint) pudding basin. Put the syrup in the bottom. Using a wooden spoon, smear the sides of the basin with syrup. Drain the juice from the can of pineapple and make it up to 300 ml (½ pint) with lemon juice and water and keep it in a saucepan to make the sauce. Arrange the pineapple rings decoratively round the greased basin and put half a cherry inside each hole. Chop remaining cherries. Soften the butter and beat in the sugar to a light and fluffy consistency. Beat in the egg, then lightly beat in the flour, lemon rind and the rest of the cherries. Mix to a soft consistency with the milk. Carefully spoon the pudding mixture into the basin, cover with greased foil, tie round the rim with string and make a string handle.

Put 1 litre (1¾ pints) water in the pressure cooker, put in the trivet and bring to the boil. Put in the pudding. Put on the lid without the weight, lower the heat and steam for 15 minutes. Then increase the heat to bring to low (5 lb) pressure. Cook for 30 minutes. Reduce pressure slowly.

Pineapple upside-down pudding

Meanwhile blend the arrowroot with a little of the fruit juice and put the rest to boil. Mix a little of the hot liquid with the blended arrowroot, then add the mixture to the fruit juice. Bring to the boil and stir until the sauce thickens. Loosen the pudding from the basin, turn it out on to a warm plate and serve with the sauce.

Apple pudding

Rhubarb, gooseberries, apricots, blackberries, blackcurrants or plums may be used instead of apples.

450 g (1 lb) cooking apples, peeled and cored
100 g (4 oz) sugar
grated rind of 1 small lemon, or 2–3 whole cloves

For suet crust pastry
225 g (8 oz) self raising flour
2·5 ml (½ level tsp) salt
100 g (4 oz) shredded suet
about 150 ml (¼ pint) cold water

Grease a 900-ml (1½-pint) pudding basin. To make the suet crust pastry, mix the dry ingredients to a soft dough with water. Knead it on a floured surface, roll out three quarters of it and line the prepared basin. Roll out the remaining pastry to form a lid. Cut the apples into even slices and mix with the sugar and flavouring. Turn the fruit into the prepared basin, damp the top edge of the pastry and put on the pastry lid. Seal the edges together well. Cover with greased foil, tie round rim with string and make a handle.

Put 1 litre (1¾ pints) water in the pressure cooker, put in the trivet and bring to the boil. Lower the pudding into cooker and put on the lid without the weight. Lower the heat and steam the pudding for 15 minutes. Then put on the weight and increase the heat to bring the cooker to low (5 lb) pressure. Cook for 40 minutes. Reduce pressure slowly. Serve the pudding with custard.

Plum duff

100 g (4 oz) self raising flour
100 g (4 oz) fresh breadcrumbs
100 g (4 oz) shredded suet
2·5 ml (½ level tsp) salt
50 g (2 oz) soft brown sugar
50 g (2 oz) sultanas
50 g (2 oz) currants
about 150 ml (¼ pint) milk
80 g (3 oz) brown butter hard sauce (see below)

Mix together all the dry ingredients in a bowl and stir in the milk to make a soft dough. Put the mixture in a greased 900-ml (1½-pint) basin, cover with greased foil, tie round rim with string and make a handle. Put 1 litre (1¾ pints) water in the pressure cooker, put in the trivet and bring the water to the boil. Lower pudding into the cooker. Put on lid without the weight and lower the heat. Steam for 15 minutes. Put on the weight and increase the heat to bring to low (5 lb) pressure. Cook for 30 minutes. Reduce pressure slowly. Turn the pudding out on to a hot dish and serve with brown butter hard sauce.

Brown butter hard sauce
40 g (1½ oz) butter
40 g (1½ oz) soft brown sugar
finely grated rind of 1 small lemon

Soften the butter and beat in the sugar and rind; cream well together, then pile the butter into a small dish and chill. Serve with suet puddings.

Rich fruit sponge

100 g (4 oz) self raising flour
25 g (1 oz) ground almonds
50 g (2 oz) white breadcrumbs
25 g (1 oz) glacé cherries, chopped
25 g (1 oz) mixed cut peel
25 g (1 oz) raisins, stoned
100 g (4 oz) butter or block margarine
100 g (4 oz) caster sugar
2 eggs
30 ml (2 tbsp) milk
brandy butter for serving (see page 97)

Grease a 900-ml (1½-pint) basin. Mix together in a bowl all the dry ingredients except the sugar. Soften the butter in a bowl and beat in the sugar until it is light and fluffy. Gradually beat in the eggs and milk. Carefully fold in the dry ingredients and mix well. Put the pudding mixture in the prepared basin, cover with greased foil, tie round the rim with string and make a handle.

Put 1 litre (1¾ pints) water in the pressure cooker, put in the trivet and bring the water to the boil. Put in the pudding. Cover with the lid without the weight, lower the heat and steam the pudding for 15 minutes. Then increase the heat to bring to low (5 lb) pressure. Cook for a further 35 minutes. Reduce the pressure slowly. Turn the pudding out on to a hot plate. Serve with brandy butter.

Golden pudding

175 g (6 oz) golden syrup
225 g (8 oz) self raising flour
2·5 ml (½ level tsp) salt
5 ml (1 level tsp) baking powder
5 ml (1 level tsp) ground ginger
100 g (4 oz) shredded suet
1 egg, beaten
60–90 ml (4–6 tbsp) milk
extra golden syrup for serving

Grease a 900-ml (1½-pint) pudding basin well and put about one third of the syrup in the bottom. Put the dry ingredients in a bowl, add the rest of the syrup and mix to a soft dough with the egg and milk. Put the mixture in the prepared basin, cover with greased foil, tie string round the rim and make a handle. Put 1 litre (1¾ pints) water in the pressure cooker, put in the trivet and bring to the boil.

Gently lower the pudding on to the trivet. Put on the lid without the weight, lower the heat and steam for 15 minutes. Then increase the heat to bring to low (5 lb) pressure. Cook for 40 minutes. Reduce pressure slowly. Take out the pudding, loosen it from the basin and turn it out on to a hot dish. Serve with golden syrup.

Christmas pudding

Christmas puddings can be made most successfully in a pressure cooker and the initial cooking can be cut down considerably. Any favourite pudding recipe can be used but the recipe below makes a good family sized pudding, sufficient for 5–6 people. It is not advisable to make a larger one, but two 600-ml (1-pint) puddings could be made instead, with one standing above the other if a high dome cooker is used. After mixing, the puddings are pre-steamed for 15–30 minutes (depending on size) to allow them to swell and rise, then they are cooked for the rest of the time at high (15 lb) pressure.

75 g (3 oz) raisins, stoned
100 g (4 oz) currants
100 g (4 oz) sultanas
25 g (1 oz) mixed cut peel
25 g (1 oz) glacé cherries, chopped
25 g (1 oz) almonds, blanched and chopped
50 g (2 oz) brown sugar
50 g (2 oz) fresh breadcrumbs
25 g (1 oz) flour
pinch of salt
50 g (2 oz) shredded suet
grated rind of ½ lemon
greated rind of ½ orange
5 ml (1 level tsp) mixed spice
2 eggs, beaten
90 ml (6 tbsp) milk

Well grease a 900-ml (1½-pint) pudding basin and have ready a piece of greased foil. Put all the prepared fruit in a bowl with the rest of the dry ingredients. Mix to a soft dough with the eggs and milk (a little extra milk may be needed to form a soft consistency). Put the pudding in the prepared basin and cover with greased greaseproof paper and greased foil. Tie round the rim and make a handle over the top with a piece of string.

Put 1·4 litres (2½ pints) water in the pressure cooker and put in the trivet. Bring the water to the boil. Lower the heat and put the pudding in the cooker. Put on the lid without the weight and steam the pudding for 30 minutes. Then increase the heat to bring to high (15 lb) pressure. Cook the pudding for 1¾ hours. Reduce pressure slowly. Remove the pudding from the cooker and take off the foil when the pudding is cold, leave grease-proof in place, cover with dry foil and store in a cool dry place until required.

To reheat the pudding when required. Put 600 ml (1 pint) water in the pressure cooker. Put in the trivet and stand the covered pudding in the cooker. Put on the lid and bring to high (15 lb) pressure. Cook for 30 minutes. Reduce pressure slowly, turn the pudding upside down on to a hot dish and serve with brandy butter (see page 97).

Chocolate crumb pudding

50 g (2 oz) cooking chocolate, broken into pieces
60 ml (4 tbsp) milk
100 g (4 oz) fresh white breadcrumbs
75 g (3 oz) butter
75 g (3 oz) caster sugar
1 large egg, separated
2·5 ml (½ tsp) vanilla essence
50 g (2 oz) self raising flour

Grease a 600-ml (1-pint) pudding basin. Put the chocolate and milk together in a small bowl, and stand it over a saucepan of hot water until the chocolate has melted. Then pour the chocolate on to the breadcrumbs in a bowl and leave to soak. Soften the butter and beat in the sugar until light and fluffy. Beat in the egg yolk, with the soaked crumbs and vanilla essence, then lightly beat in the flour with a little extra milk, if necessary, to make a soft dropping consistency. Whisk the egg white to the soft peak stage and fold it into the mixture. Spoon the pudding mixture into the prepared basin, cover with greased foil, tie round the rim with string and make a handle.

Put 1 litre (1¾ pints) water in the pressure cooker, put in the trivet and bring the water to the boil. Put in the pudding. Put on the lid without the weight, lower the heat and steam for 15 minutes. Then

Black cap pudding (see page 97)

increase the heat to bring to low (5 lb) pressure. Cook for 30 minutes. Reduce pressure slowly. Turn the pudding out on to a hot dish. Serve with hot chocolate sauce (see below).

Chocolate sauce

15 ml (1 level tbsp) cornflour
15 ml (1 level tbsp) cocoa powder
30 ml (2 level tbsp) sugar
300 ml (½ pint) milk
knob of butter

Blend the cornflour, cocoa and sugar with enough of the measured milk to give a thin cream. Heat the remaining milk with the butter until boiling and pour on to the blended mixture, stirring all the time to prevent lumps forming. Return the mixture to the pan and bring to the boil, stirring until it thickens; cook for a further 1–2 minutes.

Black cap pudding

See colour picture facing page 96

75 g (3 oz) mixed dried fruit
50 g (2 oz) soft brown sugar
15 ml (1 tbsp) melted butter
100 g (4 oz) butter or margarine, softened
100 g (4 oz) caster sugar
grated rind of ½ lemon
2 eggs
175 g (6 oz) self raising flour
30 ml (2 tbsp) milk

Grease a 900-ml (1½-pint) pudding basin. Mix together the dried fruit, brown sugar and melted butter and put the mixture in the pudding basin. Cream together the softened butter and caster sugar until light and fluffy. Beat in the lemon rind and the eggs, adding a little flour with each egg. Beat in the remaining flour and milk and mix well. Spoon the mixture into the basin and cover with greased foil. Tie string round the rim and make a handle.

Put 1 litre (1¾ pints) water in the pressure cooker with the trivet and bring the water to the boil. Lower the pudding into the cooker and put on the lid without the weight, lower the heat and

steam for 15 minutes. Then put on the weight and increase the heat to bring to low (5 lb) pressure. Cook for 30 minutes. Reduce pressure slowly. Turn the pudding out on to a hot dish and serve with brandy butter (see below) or custard.

Brandy butter

75 g (3 oz) butter
175 g (6 oz) icing sugar, sieved
45–75 ml (3–5 tbsp) brandy

Soften the butter and gradually beat in the icing sugar and brandy to taste until the mixture is light and fluffy. Pile the brandy butter into a sauceboat or dish and leave it in a cool place for 1–2 hours to harden before serving.

Lemon sponge pudding

This mixture gives a light, spongy custard type of pudding.

grated rind and juice of 1 large thin-skinned lemon
50 g (2 oz) butter
100 g (4 oz) caster sugar
2 eggs, separated
50 g (2 oz) self raising flour
300 ml (½ pint) milk

Grease a 700-ml (1¼-pint) ovenproof soufflé dish or casserole that will fit in the pressure cooker. Cream together the lemon rind, butter and sugar until pale and fluffy. Add the egg yolks and flour and beat well. Stir in the milk and 30–45 ml (2–3 tbsp) lemon juice (at this stage the mixture is likely to curdle). Whisk the egg whites to a soft peak in a bowl and fold them into the lemon mixture. Put the pudding mixture in the prepared dish or casserole. Cover lightly with a piece of greased foil.

Put 600 ml (1 pint) water in the pressure cooker, put in the trivet and bring the water to the boil. Put the pudding in the cooker. Cover with the lid without a weight, lower the heat and steam for 15 minutes. Then increase the heat to bring to low (5 lb) pressure. Cook for 30 minutes. Reduce pressure slowly. Turn out the pudding and serve straight away.

Chicken liver pâté (see page 108)

Francis's special chocolate castles

75 g (3 oz) blended white cooking fat
100 g (4 oz) soft brown sugar
100 g (4 oz) self raising flour
pinch of salt
15 ml (1 level tbsp) cocoa
2 eggs
15 ml (1 tbsp) cold water

For the topping
100 g (4 oz) cooking chocolate, broken into pieces
60 ml (4 tbsp) milk

Put all the pudding ingredients together in a bowl and beat together until well mixed. Put the mixture into eight greased dariole moulds or small cups. Put 600 ml (1 pint) water in the pressure cooker with the trivet and bring to the boil. Put the puddings in the cooker and cover with one piece of foil. Put on the lid without the weight, lower the heat and steam for 5 minutes. Then increase the heat to bring to high (15 lb) pressure. Cook for 10 minutes. Reduce pressure slowly. Take out the puddings and turn out on to a hot dish. Meanwhile melt the chocolate in the milk over a gentle heat and put a spoonful over each pudding before serving.

MAKES 8 SMALL PUDDINGS

Apple cap pudding

300 g (12 oz) cooking apples
25 g (1 oz) demerara sugar
grated rind of 1 lemon
75 g (3 oz) butter
75 g (3 oz) caster sugar
1 egg, beaten
125 g (5 oz) self raising flour
30 ml (2 tbsp) milk

Grease a 1-litre (1¾-pint) pudding basin. Peel, core and slice the apples and put them in the prepared basin. Sprinkle with demerara sugar and lemon rind. Cream the butter and sugar together in a bowl until light and fluffy. Beat in the egg and lastly lightly beat in the flour and milk to give a soft dropping consistency. Put the pudding mixture in the prepared basin and cover with greased foil. Tie round the rim with string and make a handle.

Put 1 litre (1¾ pints) water in the pressure cooker, put in the trivet and bring the water to the boil. Put in the pudding. Put on lid without the weight, lower the heat and steam for 15 minutes. Increase the heat to bring to low (5 lb) pressure. Cook for a further 40 minutes. Reduce pressure slowly. Remove the pudding and turn it out upside down on to a hot dish. Serve with custard.

Date and nut roll

100 g (4 oz) fresh breadcrumbs
100 g (4 oz) self raising flour
100 g (4 oz) shredded suet
50 g (2 oz) soft brown sugar
100 g (4 oz) dates, chopped
50 g (2 oz) chopped walnuts
about 150 ml (¼ pint) milk
brown butter hard sauce for serving

Grease a large piece of foil. Put all the dry ingredients together in a bowl and mix to a dough with the milk. The dough should be soft but firm enough to handle. Shape the dough into a sausage shape on a floured surface and put it on the foil; fold the foil loosely, so that the pudding can expand, but seal the edges tightly together. Put 1 litre (1¾ pints) water in the pressure cooker and put in the trivet. Bring the water to the boil. Stand the pudding on the trivet. Cover with the lid without the weight, lower the heat and steam the pudding for 15 minutes. Then increase the heat to bring to low (5 lb) pressure. Cook for 40 minutes. Reduce pressure slowly. Turn the pudding out on to a hot dish and serve sliced with brown butter hard sauce (see page 95).

Guide to pre-steaming and pressure cooking puddings

The cooking time varies according to the type and weight of the pudding and, to a certain extent, to the type of container in which it is cooked. If a very thick glass or china mould is used, add 10 minutes to the usual cooking time.

Approximate weight of pudding mix.	Size of basin	(Normal steaming time, i.e. not in pressure cooker)	Pre-steaming time (without weight)	Pressure cooking time
Sponge or rubbed in puddings				
450 g (1 lb)	8 darioles or 4 small cups	(40 minutes)	5 minutes	10 minutes at high (15 lb) pressure
450 g (1 lb)	700 ml (1¼ pints)	(1–1¼ hours)	15 minutes	25 minutes at low (5 lb) pressure
700 g (1½ lb)	900 ml (1½ pints)	(1¼–1½ hours)	15 minutes	30 minutes at low (5 lb) pressure
Suet pudding mixes				
450 g (1 lb)	700 ml (1¼ pints)	(1½ hours)	15 minutes	30 minutes at low (5 lb) pressure
700 g (1½ lb)	900 ml (1½ pints)	(2 hours)	15 minutes	40 minutes at low (5 lb) pressure

Suet lined puddings with a filling, such as fruit puddings, need 10 minutes less cooking time.

				Pressure cooking at high (15 lb) pressure
Christmas pudding				
450 g (1 lb)	400 ml (¾ pint)	(3–4 hours)	15 minutes	1½ hours
700 g (1½ lb)	900 ml (1½ pints)	(4–5 hours)	30 minutes	1¾ hours
1 kg (2¼ lb)	1·1 litres (2 pints)	(6 hours)	30 minutes	2¼ hours

MEALS FROM THE PRESSURE COOKER

Where cooking facilities are limited – for example, in a boat, caravan or bed sitter – a pressure cooker can be one of the most useful items of kitchen equipment. Because the cooking times are reduced, some dishes can be quickly prepared beforehand to be served cold as part of the meal and a complete main course can be cooked just before serving. This cuts down washing up of other pots and pans and avoids the need to keep food hot. The separators are useful for cooking the vegetables on these occasions.

Planning and working to a timetable is essential when cooking a complete meal in a pressure cooker. Always include one cold dish that can be prepared beforehand. Cooking times vary so try to choose foods which take the same time, remembering that some vegetables can be cut small to make them cook more quickly, or add the vegetables in separators part of the way through the cooking. Remember not to overload the cooker when cooking two or three foods together – see the recommendations on page 14. Plan the meal so that the cooker is not opened more than once, or at the most twice, during the cooking: otherwise time and fuel is wasted.

A few menus are listed below which give the recipes and timetables for completing the meal. Each menu serves four.

◆

MENU 1

*Mediterranean peppers
with crispbread or toast*

*Pork ragoût with rice
French or runner beans*

Stuffed apples with cream

◆

Preparation and cooking earlier in the day
Prepare and cook the mediterranean peppers. Leave in refrigerator to chill.

Prepare and cook the stuffed apples and leave to cool. Whip the cream and leave in the refrigerator.

Collect together all ingredients for the main course and prepare the vegetables.

About 40 minutes before the meal is required
Fry the meat and vegetables for the pork ragoût (allow about 10–12 minutes for this).

Add the other ingredients for this dish and bring to high (15 lb) pressure. Cook for 10 minutes.

Reduce pressure and put in the rice in a separator. Bring to high (15 lb) pressure and cook for 5 minutes.

Reduce pressure slowly. Arrange the pork and rice in a hot dish. Keep warm. Rinse out the pressure cooker and put in 300 ml (½ pint) water and the trivet. Put in the beans in a separator, lightly sprinkled with salt. Bring to high (15 lb) pressure and cook for 5 minutes. Reduce pressure quickly. Keep hot. Serve the first course.

Mediterranean peppers

2 medium-size red peppers, seeded and sliced
2 medium-size green peppers, seeded and sliced
2 medium-size onions, skinned and sliced
4 medium-size tomatoes, skinned and sliced
4 medium-size courgettes, washed and sliced
30 ml (2 tbsp) cooking oil
1 large clove of garlic, skinned and crushed
2·5 ml (½ level tsp) dried oregano or marjoram
150 ml (¼ pint) tomato juice
salt
freshly ground pepper
30 ml (2 tbsp) olive oil
60-g (2-oz) can of anchovies, drained
30 ml (2 tbsp) chopped parsley

Lightly fry the vegetables in the heated cooking oil in the uncovered cooker for about 5 minutes, until they are just brown. Stir in the garlic, herbs, tomato juice and seasoning. Put on the lid and bring to high (15 lb) pressure. Cook for 5 minutes. Reduce pressure quickly. Spoon the mixture into a bowl, adjust the seasoning and stir in the olive oil. Leave the vegetables to get cold and then chill. Cut half the anchovies into small pieces and stir them into the vegetable mixture. Spoon the vegetables on to 4 individual dishes, garnish the top with chopped parsley and the rest of the anchovies. Serve with crispbread or toast.

Pork ragoût with rice

2 onions, skinned and sliced
50 g (2 oz) fat
900 g (2 lb) shoulder pork, boned and cubed
2 small tomatoes, skinned and sliced
juice of 1 orange, strained
2 cloves of garlic, skinned and crushed
150 ml (¼ pint) red wine
300 ml (½ pint) stock or water
1 bayleaf
3 sage leaves
1·25 ml (¼ level tsp) chilli seasoning
salt and pepper
175 g (6 oz) long grain rice

Cook the onions until just transparent in the fat in the uncovered pressure cooker. Remove the onions and fry the pork until well browned, drain off excess fat. Return the onions to the cooker with the tomatoes, orange juice, garlic, wine, stock, herbs, chilli seasoning, salt and pepper. Put on the lid and bring to high (15 lb) pressure and cook for 10 minutes. Reduce pressure quickly.

Put the washed rice in a greased bowl or solid separator and pour on 400 ml (¾ pint) cold water, add 5 ml (1 level tsp) salt, cover with a piece of greased foil and put into the pressure cooker, standing the container on the trivet. Bring to high (15 lb) pressure. Cook for a further 5 minutes. Reduce pressure slowly. Fluff the rice with a fork and serve in a hot dish surrounding the pork.

Stuffed apples

4 medium-size cooking apples
25 g (1 oz) butter
25 g (1 oz) soft brown sugar
50 g (2 oz) stoned dates
5 ml (1 level tsp) grated lemon rind

Wash and core the apples and make a cut through the skin around the centre of each apple. Soften the butter and work in the sugar, dates and lemon rind. Stuff the mixture into the cavity of each apple. Put the apples in an ovenproof dish that will fit easily in the pressure cooker or use a suitable separator.

Cover the container lightly with greased foil. Put the trivet in cooker, pour in 300 ml (½ pint) water and stand the dish on the trivet. Put on the lid and bring to high (15 lb) pressure. Cook for 4 minutes. Reduce pressure slowly. Serve hot or cold with whipped cream.

◆————————————————◆

MENU 2

Spring vegetable soup

Trout maître d'hôtel
New potatoes – Peas à la française

Gooseberry fool

◆————————————————◆

Preparation and cooking earlier in the day
Cook the gooseberries and leave to cool. Purée them in readiness for making the fool.

Collect together all ingredients for the other dishes. Prepare the vegetables. Make maître d'hôtel butter and keep it in the refrigerator. Brown the almonds.

Make the gooseberry fool and leave it in individual glasses to chill.

Wash and clean the trout and remove the heads if necessary.

About 15 minutes before the meal is required
Make the spring vegetable soup. Cook at high (15 lb) pressure for 5 minutes. Serve the soup. Rinse out the cooker.

Put 300 ml (½ pint) water in the pressure cooker with the trivet. Wrap the prepared fish in foil and place on the trivet. Put vegetables into separate separators, sprinkle with salt and cover with greased foil. Pressure cook at high (15 lb) pressure for 5 minutes. If your pressure cooker is not large enough to cook everything together, cook the potatoes separately.

Reduce pressure quickly. Arrange the fish on a hot plate, sprinkle with almonds and put on the maître d'hôtel butter.

Spring vegetable soup

6–8 spring onions, washed and chopped
100 g (4 oz) new carrots, washed and sliced
50 g (2 oz) young turnip, peeled and diced
8–12 pieces of asparagus, cut in 2·5-cm (1-in lengths)
50 g (2 oz) shelled peas
bayleaf
25 g (1 oz) long grain rice
700 ml (1¼ pints) rich chicken stock
salt and freshly ground pepper

Put all the prepared vegetables in the pressure cooker with the bayleaf, rice and stock. Season. Bring to the boil uncovered and stir well. Put on the lid and bring to high (15 lb) pressure. Cook for 5 minutes. Reduce pressure quickly. Remove the bayleaf and adjust seasoning. Pour into individual heated soup bowls and cover if possible. Serve with toast or crispbread.

Trout maître d'hôtel

butter
25 g (1 oz) flaked almonds
4 trout about 150–175 g (5–6 oz) each
salt
freshly ground pepper
60 ml (4 tbsp) dry white wine
lemon wedges
sprigs of parsley
maître d'hôtel butter (see page 103)

Melt 25 g (1 oz) butter and lightly fry the almonds until golden brown. Reserve to use later. Wash and clean the trout thoroughly – if they are not too large for pressure cooker leave the heads on, otherwise remove the heads. Butter four pieces of foil and place the fish on them, sprinkle with salt and pepper. Spoon 15 ml (1 tbsp) wine over each. Fold the foil round each fish to make a neat parcel, and seal the ends. Put the trivet in the cooker and pour in 300 ml (½ pint) water. Put the fish on the trivet or in a flat separator and put on the lid. Bring to high (15 lb) pressure. Cook for 5 minutes. Reduce pressure quickly. Remove the fish and open the foil. Serve the fish head to tail on a hot dish, garnished with lemon wedges and parsley. Put a portion of maître d'hôtel butter on each fish before serving and sprinkle with browned almonds.

Maître d'hôtel butter

50 g (2 oz) butter
salt
freshly ground pepper
1·25 ml (¼ level tsp) finely grated lemon rind
30 ml (2 tbsp) chopped parsley

Soften the butter on a plate with a round bladed knife and work in the seasoning and flavourings. Shape into 4 flat cakes or balls and chill.

Peas à la française

¼ lettuce, washed and shredded
6 spring onions, washed and chopped
sprig of parsley and mint tied together
350 g (12 oz) shelled fresh peas
150 ml (¼ pint) water
25 g (1 oz) butter
salt and pepper
5 ml (1 level tsp) sugar

Put the lettuce, onions, herbs, peas, water, butter and salt into a separator or ovenproof bowl. Cover the container with foil. Pour 300 ml (½ pint) water in the pressure cooker, put in the trivet and stand the peas on it. Put on the lid and bring to high (15 lb) pressure. Cook for 5 minutes. Reduce pressure quickly. Remove the herbs and sprinkle the peas with pepper and sugar before serving.

Gooseberry fool

350 g (12 oz) fresh gooseberries, washed
50 g (2 oz) sugar
142-ml (5-fl oz) carton of double cream
1 egg white
4 glacé cherries
shortbread or ginger biscuits

Put the gooseberries in a separator or ovenproof dish, sprinkle with the sugar and cover with foil. Put the trivet in the pressure cooker, add 300 ml (½ pint) water, and stand the separator or dish on the trivet. Put on the lid and bring to high (15 lb) pressure. Cook for 4 minutes. Reduce pressure slowly. Purée the fruit through a sieve. Leave the purée to cool – there should be about 300 ml (½ pint). When the purée is cold, whip the cream and egg white together until light and frothy and fold it into the gooseberry purée. Put the fool in individual glasses and top each with a glacé cherry. Serve with shortbread or ginger biscuits.

If an electric blender is to be used to purée the fruit, top and tail the gooseberries before cooking.

◆

MENU 3

Vichyssoise soup

Steak and mushroom pudding
Sliced carrots and Cauliflower sprigs

Caramel custard

◆

Preparation and cooking earlier in the day

Make the caramel custard. If preferred, this can be done the day before. Leave the custard to cool in the tin until required.

Make the soup earlier in the day and chill.

Prepare and cook the meat filling for the pudding, put aside to cool until required.

Collect together the ingredients for the pudding, prepare the vegetables, break the cauliflower into sprigs.

About 45 minutes before the meal is required

Make the suet crust pastry, line the basin and make the meat pudding.

Put the pudding to steam for 15 minutes.

Bring cooker to low (5 lb) pressure and cook for a further 30 minutes. Meanwhile turn out the caramel custard. Whip the cream, if using, and keep it in refrigerator. Reduce pressure slowly, remove the pudding and keep it warm in the basin and rinse out the cooker.

Put 300 ml (½ pint) water in the cooker and put in the trivet. Put the carrots and cauliflower sprigs in the vegetable separators, sprinkle with salt. Put the remaining gravy in a small basin, cover it with foil and stand it in the pressure cooker to reheat, put in the vegetables. Put on the lid.

Bring to high (15 lb) pressure and cook for 3 minutes. Keep vegetables hot.

Vichyssoise soup

3 leeks, trimmed, sliced and washed
1 onion, skinned and sliced
50 g (2 oz) butter or margarine
1 large potato, peeled and sliced
600 ml (1 pint) chicken stock
bayleaf
salt and pepper
90 ml (6 tbsp) single cream
chopped chives or parsley for garnish

Lightly fry the leeks and onion in the fat in the uncovered pressure cooker for 2–3 minutes until softened but not browned. Stir in the potato, stock, bayleaf and seasoning. Put on the lid and bring to high (15 lb) pressure. Cook for 5 minutes, then reduce pressure quickly. Remove the bayleaf and sieve the soup or purée it in an electric blender. Stir in the cream, adjust seasoning and chill. Sprinkle with chopped chives or parsley before serving.

Steak and mushroom pudding

450 g (1 lb) chuck or shoulder steak
15 ml (1 level tbsp) seasoned flour
1 onion, skinned and chopped
100 g (4 oz) mushrooms, sliced
300 ml (½ pint) stock or water

For the suet crust pastry
225 g (8 oz) self raising flour
2·5 g (½ level tsp) salt
100 g (4 oz) shredded suet
about 150 ml (¼ pint) cold water

Cut the meat into 2·5-cm (1-in) pieces and toss it in the seasoned flour. Put the meat in the pressure cooker with the onion, mushrooms and stock. Put on the lid and bring to high (15 lb) pressure. Cook for 15 minutes. Reduce pressure quickly. Leave the meat filling to cool.

Grease a 900-ml (1 ½-pint) pudding basin. Make the suet crust pastry by mixing the dry ingredients to a soft dough with water. Knead the dough on a floured surface, roll out three quarters of it and line the pudding basin. Roll out the rest of the dough to make a lid. Damp the top edge of the pastry and spoon the meat filling into the prepared basin, leaving about half the gravy to use later. Put on the pastry lid, seal the edges and cover with greased foil. Tie string round the rim and then over the basin to make a handle. Put the trivet in the cooker, pour in 1·1 litres (2 pints) water and bring to the boil. Lower the pudding into cooker. Put on the lid without the weight and lower the heat so that the cooker steams gently but constantly for 15 minutes. Then put on the weight and increase the heat to bring to low (5 lb) pressure. Continue to cook for 30 minutes. Reduce pressure slowly. Serve the pudding with the extra gravy, reheated.

*Steak and mushroom pudding;
Caramel custard*

Caramel custard

100 g (4 oz) sugar
150 ml (¼ pint) water
30 ml (2 tbsp) lemon juice
butter
3 eggs
25 g (1 oz) caster sugar
400 ml (¾ pint) milk
**142-ml (5-fl oz) carton of double cream or biscuits
  for serving**

Put the sugar with the water in a small pan and dissolve it over gentle heat. When the sugar is completely dissolved, bring the syrup to the boil and let it boil until the sugar caramelises. When it is a good golden brown, remove the pan from heat and slowly add the lemon juice; allow the caramel to dissolve in it. If necessary, return the pan to low heat. Pour the caramel in a warmed plain 15-cm (6-in) cake tin or mould and turn the tin until the bottom is completely covered with caramel. When the caramel is firm, butter the sides of the tin above the caramel coating.

Put the milk in a pan to heat. Whisk together the eggs and sugar in a bowl and stir in the heated milk; mix well, then pour the custard in the prepared tin and cover with foil. Put 300 ml (½ pint) water in the pressure cooker and put in the trivet. Stand the custard on the trivet and put on the lid. Bring to high (15 lb) pressure. Cook for 5 minutes. Reduce pressure slowly. Leave the custard to get quite cold before turning it out on to a serving dish. Serve with whipped cream or biscuits.

MENU 4

Soused herrings

*Pot roasted chicken with
spring vegetables*

Rice imperial with apricot sauce

Preparation and cooking earlier in the day
Prepare and cook the soused herrings, leave in a cool place, then chill.

Make the creamed rice for the rice imperial and leave to cool. Make the apricot purée and sauce, in readiness for the meal.

Prepare the chicken and vegetables for the main course.

Complete the rice imperial and leave to set in a cool place.

About 35 minutes before the meal is required
Fry the chicken until brown and drain off the fat (allow 10 minutes for this).

Put the chicken back in pressure cooker on the trivet with the sliced onion, carrot, stock etc. Put on the lid and bring to high (15 lb) pressure, cook for 15 minutes.

Turn out the rice imperial.

Reduce cooker pressure quickly. Add all other vegetables, sprinkled with salt. Put on the lid and bring to high (15 lb) pressure again for 6 minutes.

Soused herrings

4 small herrings, cleaned and beheaded
salt and pepper
1 medium-size onion, skinned and sliced

1 bayleaf
4 peppercorns
150 ml (¼ pint) vinegar
150 ml (¼ pint) water
shredded lettuce
4 gherkins

Split the herrings open on the underside. Put them on a board, cut side down and press lightly with the fingers along the middle of the back to loosen the bones. Turn the fish over and ease the backbone away from the flesh, removing any other small bones. Remove the roe at the same time. Sprinkle the fish with salt and pepper, put back the roe, roll up the fish from the head end and secure with a cocktail stick. Put the herrings in an ovenproof dish with the onion, bayleaf, peppercorns, vinegar and water. Cover with greased foil. Put 300 ml (½ pint) water in the pressure cooker, put in the trivet and stand the dish on it. Put on the lid and bring to high (15 lb) pressure. Cook for 5 minutes. Reduce pressure quickly. Remove the dish from the cooker and leave to cool. When cold, arrange the soused herrings on individual plates with lettuce and garnish with gherkin fans. Serve with brown bread and butter.

Pot roasted chicken

Cooking time for chicken:
6–8 minutes per 450 g (1 lb)

1 chicken about 1·1 kg (2 ½ lb) with giblets
25 g (1 oz) butter
15 ml (1 tbsp) oil
300 ml (½ pint) water
2 onions, skinned and sliced
1 large carrot, pared and sliced
bouquet garni
salt and pepper
225 g (8 oz) young carrots, washed
100 g (4 oz) small whole turnips, washed
8 shallots, skinned
8–12 small new potatoes, scraped
30 ml (2 tbsp) chopped parsley
30 ml (2 tbsp) cornflour, optional

Weigh the chicken and calculate cooking time.

Brown the chicken all over in the heated butter and oil in the uncovered pressure cooker. Drain off the fat and put the trivet in the cooker. Pour in the water, add the giblets, sliced onions and carrot, the bouquet garni and seasoning. Put on the lid and bring to high (15 lb) pressure. Cook for about 20 minutes.

Six minutes before the end of the calculated cooking time, reduce the pressure quickly and add the other vegetables, sprinkled with salt. Bring to high (15 lb) pressure again and cook for a further 6 minutes. Reduce pressure quickly. Put the chicken with the vegetables in a hot dish sprinkled with parsley. If wished, thicken the gravy by blending 30 ml (2 level tbsp) cornflour with a little water, then stir in a little of the hot gravy. Add the mixture to the cooker, return it to the heat and bring to the boil, stirring until the gravy thickens. Serve the gravy separately.

Rice imperial

25 g (1 oz) butter
568 ml (1 pint) milk
50 g (2 oz) pudding rice
50 g (2 oz) sugar
30 ml (2 tbsp) white wine
15 ml (3 level tsp) powdered gelatine
25 g (1 oz) angelica
25 g (1 oz) glacé cherries
142-ml (5-fl oz) carton of whipping cream
300 ml (½ pint) apricot sauce (see below)

Put the butter in the pressure cooker and heat gently so that it melts and greases the base. Pour in the milk, bring it to the boil in the uncovered cooker, then stir in the rice and sugar. Stir well and bring to the boil, then lower the heat until it simmers. Put on the lid and when the steam is escaping allow the cooker to come to high (15 lb) pressure slowly, then cook for 5 minutes. Reduce pressure slowly. Put the rice in a bowl to cool. Put the wine in a small bowl and sprinkle over the gelatine, leave it to stand for about 5 minutes, then dissolve (see Apricot cream page 111). Cut the angelica and cherries into small pieces, blend with the cold creamy rice and stir in the dissolved gelatine. When the rice is nearly set, stir in the whipped cream, mix lightly and spoon it into a 600 ml (1 pint) ring mould. Leave in a cool place to set. Turn out the rice and serve with apricot sauce.

Apricot sauce
300 ml (½ pint) boiling water
100 g (4 oz) dried apricots
50 g (2 oz) sugar
30 ml (2 tbsp) lemon juice

Pour the boiling water over the apricots and soak for 30 minutes. Drain the apricots and put them in the pressure cooker with 300 ml (½ pint) water, the sugar and lemon juice. Put on the lid and bring to high (15 lb) pressure. Cook for 10 minutes. Reduce pressure quickly. Sieve the apricots or purée them in an electric blender. Leave the apricot purée to cool. Thin it down a little with sugar syrup or white wine if it is too thick.

♦

MENU 5

Chicken liver pâté
Stuffed plaice fillets tartare
Spinach and potatoes
Cherry sponge charlotte

♦

Preparation and cooking earlier in the day
Make the pâté earlier in the day or preferably the previous day. Make the tartare sauce.

Collect together all ingredients for the cherry sponge charlotte.

Prepare the potatoes and make the stuffing for the fish fillets. Stuff the fillets and leave them ready wrapped in foil in a cool place.

About 30 minutes before the meal is required
Make the cherry sponge charlotte and leave to soak 5 minutes. Put 300 ml (½ pint) water in pressure cooker with trivet. Put the pudding to cook in the pressure cooker at high (15 lb) pressure for 15 minutes. Reduce pressure slowly. Remove pudding and allow to stand until required.

Put the fish on the trivet in the cooker. Put the frozen spinach, cut into cubes, into a separator and potatoes in another separator. Put to cook.

Chicken liver pâté

1 medium-size onion, skinned and chopped
1 large clove of garlic, skinned and crushed
75 g (3 oz) butter
450 g (1 lb) chicken livers, chopped
1 bayleaf
45 ml (3 tbsp) sherry
salt and pepper
15 ml (1 level tbsp) tomato paste
15 ml (1 tbsp) double cream
parsley sprigs

Lightly fry the onion and crushed garlic in the butter in the uncovered pressure cooker until it starts changing colour and is slightly soft. Remove it and put it in a solid container or ovenproof dish. Toss the livers in the remaining fat until they are just firm on the outside, then put them with the onions and add the bayleaf. Rinse out the cooker with the sherry, removing any bits clinging to the pan, and pour it over the livers. Add the seasoning and tomato paste, and cover with foil.

Wash the cooker, pour in 300 ml (½ pint) water and put in the trivet. Stand the container on the trivet, put on the lid of the cooker and bring to high (15 lb) pressure. Cook for 5 minutes. Reduce pressure quickly and remove the container. Remove the bayleaf. Sieve the liver mixture or purée it in an electric blender until it is smooth. Stir in the cream and adjust the seasoning. Spoon the mixture into four to six individual dishes and leave in a cool place to set firmly. Garnish with parsley sprigs and serve with hot toast and butter.
SERVES 4–6

Stuffed plaice fillets tartare

8 fillets of plaice
salt and pepper
1 medium-size onion, skinned and finely chopped
25 g (1 oz) butter
50 g (2 oz) mushrooms, finely chopped
15 ml (1 tbsp) chopped parsley

For the tartare sauce

150 ml (¼ pint) mayonnaise
5 ml (1 level tsp) chopped chives
10 ml (2 level tsp) chopped capers
10 ml (2 level tsp) chopped gherkins
15 ml (1 tbsp) lemon juice

Mix the ingredients for the sauce together and leave to stand at least 1 hour to allow flavours to blend before using.

Remove the skin from the fillets and put the fish, skinned side uppermost, on a board; sprinkle with salt and pepper. Lightly fry the onion in the butter in a small pan until it is just soft and slightly browned. Add the mushrooms and cook for a few minutes, then mix in the parsley and seasoning. Divide the mixture between the fish fillets and fold each into three. Put them on buttered foil, or in an open buttered ovenproof dish that will fit into the pressure cooker. Sprinkle with a little extra seasoning. Fold the foil into a neat parcel. Put the fish on the trivet in the cooker. Pour in 300 ml (½ pint) water and put on the lid. Bring to high (15 lb) pressure. Cook for 4 minutes. Reduce pressure quickly. Carefully arrange the fish on a hot dish. Serve the sauce separately.

Cherry sponge charlotte

butter
50 g (2 oz) glacé cherries, halved
25 g (1 oz) angelica, cut up
25 g (1 oz) large stoned raisins
16 boudoir biscuits
90 ml (6 tbsp) sherry
3 eggs, beaten
50 g (2 oz) caster sugar
300 ml (½ pint) milk
142-ml (5-fl oz) carton of single cream

Butter a 600-ml (1-pint) charlotte tin or 12·5-cm (5-in) cake tin. Arrange the cherries on the bottom with the angelica and raisins. Trim off the rounded ends of the boudoir biscuits and reserve. Dip the biscuits in the sherry, and arrange them round the sides of the tin so that they fit snugly together. Put the remaining trimmings in the prepared tin. Whisk the sugar and eggs together in a bowl until light and creamy. Warm the milk and cream in a saucepan almost to boiling point and whisk it into the eggs and sugar; add any remaining sherry. Pour the custard into the prepared tin, allow to stand for about 5 minutes, then cover with a piece of buttered foil.

Put the trivet in the pressure cooker and pour in 300 ml (½ pint) water. Stand the pudding on the trivet, put on the lid and bring to high (15 lb) pressure. Cook for 15 minutes. Reduce pressure slowly. Allow pudding to stand for a short while before turning it out on to a hot dish.

---◆---

MENU 6

Chilled prawn bisque

Ragoût of lamb with rice
Sliced carrots

Apricot cream

---◆---

Preparation and cooking earlier
Make and chill the prawn bisque.

Make the apricot purée for the apricot cream and cool it.

Prepare the lamb and vegetables.

Complete the apricot cream and leave it in a cool place to set.

About 30 minutes before the meal is required
Fry the meat and spices in the pressure cooker (allow about 10 minutes).

Add other ingredients for the ragoût and put on the lid, bring to high (15 lb) pressure and cook for 15 minutes.

Reduce pressure quickly and put in the rice and sliced carrots in separators. Bring to high pressure and cook for 5 minutes. Reduce pressure slowly.

Turn out the apricot cream ready for serving and whip the extra cream.

Chilled prawn bisque

1 medium-size onion, skinned and sliced
25 g (1 oz) butter
450 g (1 lb) tomatoes, skinned and sliced *or*
    425-g (15-oz) can of tomatoes
300 ml (½ pint) chicken stock
15 ml (1 level tbsp) tomato paste
1 cap of canned pimiento
salt
freshly ground pepper
pinch of sugar
15 ml (1 level tbsp) cornflour
15 ml (1 tbsp) sherry
50 g (2 oz) shelled prawns, chopped
30 ml (2 tbsp) cream, lightly whipped

Lightly fry the onion in the butter in the uncovered pressure cooker until just tender. Add the tomatoes with juice, stock, paste, pimiento, seasonings and sugar. Put on the lid and bring to high (15 lb) pressure. Cook for 5 minutes. Reduce pressure quickly. Sieve the mixture or purée it in an electric blender. If using an electric blender, sieve after to remove tomato pips. Return it to the cooker to reheat. Blend the cornflour to a smooth cream with the sherry and stir in some of the hot liquid. Add the mixture to the cooker, bring to the boil uncovered, stirring until the liquid thickens. Remove the cooker from the heat and allow to cool. When cold, stir in the chopped prawns and cream and chill before serving.

Ragoût of lamb with rice

1 shoulder of lamb, boned weight about 550 g (1¼ lb)
50 g (2 oz) butter or margarine
2 medium-size onions, skinned and sliced
5 ml (1 level tsp) ground coriander
2·5 ml (½ level tsp) ground ginger
1·25 ml (¼ level tsp) ground cinnamon
1·25 ml (¼ level tsp) ground cardamom
300 ml (½ pint) stock or water
salt and pepper
1 clove of garlic, skinned and crushed
350 g (12 oz) tomatoes, skinned and chopped
175 g (6 oz) long grain rice
400 ml (¾ pint) water
141-g (5-oz) carton of yoghurt

Cut the lamb into 2·5-cm (1-in) pieces and fry in the fat in the uncovered pressure cooker until it is well browned. Remove the meat from the cooker and fry the onion until just tender, then stir in the spices and cook for a further 2–3 minutes. Remove excess fat. Return the meat to the cooker, stir in the stock, seasoning, garlic and tomatoes. Put on the lid and bring to high (15 lb) pressure. Cook for 15 minutes. Put the rice into a buttered solid separator or ovenproof container, pour on the water and add salt; cover with greased foil. Reduce pressure quickly. Place the trivet over the meat and put the container of rice on the trivet. Bring to high (15 lb) pressure again and cook for a further 5 minutes. Reduce pressure slowly. Fluff the rice with a fork.

Stir the yoghurt into the ragoût before serving. Serve the rice separately.

Apricot cream

175 g (6 oz) dried apricots
50 g (2 oz) sugar
30 ml (2 tbsp) sherry or white wine
15 ml (3 level tsp) powdered gelatine
142-ml (5-fl oz) carton of whipping cream
extra cream for serving

Pour boiling water over the apricots and leave them to soak for at least 1 hour. Drain the apricots and put them in the pressure cooker with the sugar and 300 ml (½ pint) water. Put on the lid, bring to pressure and cook for 15 minutes. Reduce pressure and sieve the fruit or purée it in an electric blender. Make it up to 400 ml (¾ pint) with water or other fruit juice. Leave it to cool.

Put the wine in a small bowl, sprinkle over the gelatine, leave for a few minutes, then stand the bowl in a saucepan of hot water until the gelatine dissolves. Stir the dissolved gelatine into the cold apricot purée and keep stirring until the mixture is nearly set. Whip the cream and fold it into the mixture. Pour the apricot cream into a 600 ml (1 pint) mould and leave to set firmly. Turn out the apricot cream and serve with extra whipped cream.

FREEZING FROM THE PRESSURE COOKER

A pressure cooker is especially useful when cooking for the freezer as larger quantities can be cooked at the same time. It should be remembered, however, that the pressure cooker must not be more than half full. Nevertheless, the pressure cooker can be used several times in the period it would take to cook a casserole in the oven.

Likewise time and fuel can be saved by using the pressure cooker for reheating frozen foods. Soups, stews, casseroles, curries, fish, fruit and vegetables can all be cooked from their frozen state in a very short time but they should be broken or cut into smaller pieces (or packed by the free-flow method) before being cooked. It would not be worth using a pressure cooker to cook just one frozen vegetable. But when two or three types of vegetable are cooked at the same time, or a frozen vegetable is added to the cooker to complete a meal, there is a saving in fuel.

Bulk cooking for the freezer
If the cooker is large enough, double or treble the quantities for soups, stews or any gravy dishes. Only a little more time is needed to prepare these increased quantities and the cooking time remains the same. Make the dishes in the usual way but observe the following recommendations:

1. Use seasoning sparingly.
2. Use shallow rather than deep dishes.
3. Make the sauce or gravy thinner than usual.

Smaller packs are more convenient for reheating, especially if this is to be done in the pressure cooker. To ensure that you get the best out of frozen cooked food, use it within two months.

Fruit for the freezer
There is little advantage in freezing whole cooked fruit unless it is to use a glut of fruit or windfalls which must be used immediately. Damaged fruit can be made into a purée and this is an economical way of using it. Make purées as described on pages 89–91; pack them when cold in the usual way.

Citrus fruits can be frozen whole. This is a useful method of storing Seville oranges if it is not convenient to make marmalade at the time of purchase. It is best to cook them from the frozen state as recommended in the marmalade recipe on page 120.

Blanching vegetables for the freezer
Blanching is essential when preparing vegetables for the freezer, as it destroys the enzymes present and ensures the preservation of the flavour, colour and texture of the vegetables. It is particularly important if the food is to be stored a long time. Accurate timing is essential when blanching vegetables, and it is useful to have a pinger timer available.

General guidelines for blanching vegetables in the pressure cooker
1. Prepare the vegetables according to type (see chart). Freeze only young tender fresh vegetables.
2. Put the trivet in the pressure cooker.
3. Put 300 ml (½ pint) water (unless the manufacturers state that less may be used) into the cooker.
4. Bring the water to the boil, uncovered.
5. Put the vegetables in separators, blanching baskets or in muslin bags for easier handling and place them on the trivet in the cooker.
6. Put on the lid and bring to medium (10 lb) pressure. Blanch vegetables for the recommended time (see chart). It is most important to ensure that the timing is accurately observed, as it is so short and over-blanching would spoil the vegetables.
7. Reduce pressure quickly as soon as the blanching time is reached, and remove the vegetables.
8. Immerse the blanched vegetables in iced water to cool them quickly.
9. When cold, drain the vegetables well, pat dry and pack in bags or other containers. Make only

small packs of vegetables – never more than 450 g (1 lb).

10. Fast freeze.

Cooking raw meat

Research has shown that meat has a better flavour when cooked directly from its frozen state, although sometimes it can be a little tougher to eat. Cut up frozen meat prepared for stews or casseroles can be cooked direct from the freezer, but it is difficult to brown the meat as the water in it spurts into the fat. Add 5 minutes per 450 g (1 lb) to the usual pressure cooking time.

Large joints for pot roasts, boiled or braised dishes are not suitable for pressure cooking direct from the freezer as the heat would not penetrate the thick part of the joint before the outer edge was cooked.

Likewise, whole chickens should not be cooked straight from the frozen state, as they would not be cooked throughout in the time. Portions or joints of frozen chicken can be stewed or braised; add 5 minutes to the usual pressure cooking time.

Reheating cooked meat

Casseroles, stews and curries can all be reheated in a pressure cooker from frozen. Ensure that they are packed into the freezer in suitable containers so that they can be removed from the containers and put into ovenproof dishes or straight into the pressure cooker for reheating. Reheat as follows:

1. Break or cut the pack into smaller pieces.

2. Put 300 ml (½ pint) water in the pressure cooker with the trivet.

3. Either stand the container on the trivet or put the frozen food, unwrapped, in a solid separator.

4. Put on the lid and bring to high (15 lb) pressure.

5. For food in its container, heat for 8–10 minutes, plus extra time if the dish is thick. For food in a solid separator, heat for 6–8 minutes.

6. Reduce pressure slowly.

Cooking raw fish

Most fish is best cooked from its frozen state. This is sometimes not practical for certain recipes where the fillets have to be rolled or folded, so that

it is worth remembering to prepare the fish for freezing in the way it is to be used later.

Reheating soups

Using a pressure cooker to reheat frozen soups is a considerable saving in time. Reheat as follows:

1. Remove polythene bag or wrapping beforehand.

2. If not frozen in cubes or small amounts saw or break the frozen soup into small pieces. Put into separator or container.

3. Put 300 ml (½ pint) water in the pressure cooker with the trivet. Stand the separator or container on the trivet.

4. Put on the lid and bring to high (15 lb) pressure.

5. Reheat the soup for 7–8 minutes.

6. Reduce pressure slowly.

Cooking frozen vegetables

All vegetables can be cooked from their frozen state. It is advisable to break any solid blocks into two or three pieces before putting them in the separators. This ensures that the heat penetrates right through quickly and evenly. See the chart on pages 114–115 for cooking times for frozen vegetables. It is important to cook the vegetables for the correct time, as they overcook very quickly.

Cooking frozen fruit

Tip the fruit in a container or solid separator to ensure that the juices will be contained. Add sugar if required. Put the trivet in the pressure cooker, pour in 300 ml (½ pint) water and bring to high (15 lb) pressure. Cook for 2–3 minutes, according to variety. Reduce pressure slowly.

Boil-in-the-bag foods

Boil-in-the-bag frozen foods are a useful stand-by, whether you freeze them yourself or buy them in a shop. GHI is often asked if using a pressure cooker in conjunction with these would shorten the cooking time but the answer is a definite *no*. The boil-in-the-bag packs may well contain air and the pressure built up inside the cooker could cause this to expand and burst the bag.

Guide to blanching and cooking frozen vegetables in the pressure cooker

	Preparation	Blanching time at medium (10 lb) pressure	Final cooking from frozen in pressure cooker at high (15 lb) pressure.
Asparagus	Grade into thick and thin stems. Wash in cold water.	Bring to pressure only	thick stems 3 minutes thin stems 1 minute
Beans broad	Shell.	1 minute	3 minutes
French	Wash and trim.	Bring to pressure only	4 minutes
runner	String and slice thickly.	Bring to pressure only	4 minutes
Beetroot	Wash, scald and rub off skin. Slice.	7 minutes	5 minutes
Broccoli, purple and white	Trim off any woody parts and large leaves. Wash in salted water, divide into spears.	1 minute	4 minutes
Brussels sprouts	Use small compact heads. Remove outer leaves and wash thoroughly.	1 minute	4 minutes
Carrots	Scrape and slice. Leave small young ones whole.	2 minutes	4 minutes
Cauliflower	Wash, break into florets. Add lemon juice to blanching water to keep them white.	1 minute	4 minutes
Celeriac	Wash, trim, peel and cube.	1 minute	4 minutes

	Preparation	Blanching time at medium (10 lb) pressure	Final cooking from frozen in pressure cooker at high (15 lb) pressure.
Celery	Trim, wash and remove any strings. Chop, keep small hearts whole.	chopped, 2 minutes hearts, 3 minutes	3 minutes 4 minutes
Corn on the cob	Remove husks and 'silks'.	small, 2 minutes; large, 3 minutes	5 minutes; 6 minutes
Courgettes	Wash and trim. Slice. Leave small ones whole.	sliced, bring to pressure only whole, 2 minutes	2 minutes 3 minutes
Leeks	Cut off tops and roots; remove coarse outside leaves. Slice and wash well.	1 minute	2 minutes
Peas	Shell.	1 minute	3 minutes
Peppers	Wash well, remove stems, seeds and membranes. Halve or slice.	halved, 1 minute sliced, 1 minute	4 minutes 3 minutes
Potatoes, new	Wash, scrape and leave whole.	2 minutes	5 minutes
Spinach	Use young leaves. Wash thoroughly under running water, drain.	bring to pressure only	2 minutes

JAMS, JELLIES, MARMALADES AND CHUTNEYS

Home preserves such as jams, jellies, marmalades and chutneys, can all be made successfully using a pressure cooker. Only the preliminary softening of the fruit is done in the cooker, so soft fruits, such as raspberries and strawberries, are not included as they can be quickly prepared in the usual way. It is only worth preserving if the fruit and vegetables are available fresh and reasonably priced.

When making jams and jellies it is necessary to pre-cook the fruits in order to soften the skin and break down the cells to extract the pectin which is the setting agent. In most cases, a certain amount of water is needed to prevent the fruit from burning. Less water is required when using a pressure cooker as there is no evaporation. Recipes can be adapted by reducing the amount of added water by half, but never have less than 150 ml (¼ pint) water in the cooker.

Some fruits, such as, rhubarb, cherries and pears, are low in pectin. Other fruits, such as cooking apples, gooseberries, damsons, currants and citrus fruits, have a high pectin content. When making jam from the low pectin fruits, it is necessary to add extra acid or mix them with a high pectin fruit in order to have a good set.

Marmalade can be made from a variety of citrus fruits although the most popular are Seville oranges. These are only available here in January and February, but they can be frozen for use later (see Freezing Chapter, page 112). For marmalade, the peel and pith of the fruit are precooked with the pips, which provide the pectin. Extra acid is also added to ensure a good set. Marmalade making is usually a long process, but pressure cooking cuts soaking and cooking time.

General instructions for making chutney

The vegetables and spices for chutneys are precooked in order to blend the flavours and soften the vegetables, and considerable time is saved when this is done in the pressure cooker.

After this preliminary cooking remove the pan from the heat before adding sugar to the precooked vegetables. Stir until the sugar is completely dissolved. The chutney is then boiled in the open cooker to the correct consistency. As vegetables are low in pectin, chutney does not set as jam does; it is the driving off of excess liquid through boiling that gives chutney its thick consistency. It is therefore important to do this final cooking in an uncovered pan to permit evaporation.

Leave the chutney to mature for at least 3 months before using.

Potting and covering

When the chutney has a thick consistency and there is no excess liquid, remove it from the heat and let it cool for about 10 minutes.

Ladle the chutney into clean, dry, warm jars. Cover when cold with one of the following:

a) metal or Bakelite caps with a vinegar-proof lining
b) greaseproof paper, then a round of muslin dipped in melted wax or fat
c) preserving skin 'Porosan' (sold in rolls) or vinegar-proof paper.

General instructions for making jam and marmalade

Preparation and pre-cooking

Choose fresh and slightly under-ripe fruit.

Prepare the fruit as for normal cooking methods or as the recipe suggests. Pre-cook the fruit as directed in the recipe.

Adding Sugar

The pan is now used as an ordinary saucepan. Sugar is used as a preservative to ensure a long shelf life. Granulated sugar is suitable and economical for jam making; refined cane and beet sugar give equal results.

If the sugar is warmed before being added to the

cooked fruit it dissolves more quickly and does not cool the fruit so much, but this is not essential and is not always practical.

Sugar is always added after the pre-cooking as it tends to harden the fruit skins if added before.

After the sugar is added to the pre-cooked fruit it must be completely dissolved before the fruit is re-boiled. The jam should be boiled quickly after this until setting point is reached; this varies from 3 to 20 minutes according to kind and quantity.

Test for setting
Setting point is reached when the jam has boiled to 221°F (104°C) on a sugar thermometer. This is the most accurate method to use, but if a thermometer is not available try one of the following testing methods:

FLAKE TEST: Stir the preserve with a wooden spoon, then twist the spoon until a little of the preserve clings to it as it cools slightly. Setting point is reached when the preserve partially sets on the spoon and drops off in flakes.

SAUCER TEST: Spoon a little of the preserve on to a saucer and leave it in a cool place. The surface should set and wrinkle when setting point has been reached.

Potting and covering
Remove the preserve from the heat immediately setting point is reached and remove any scum that has formed. Allow the preserve to settle and cool slightly before potting. In the case of marmalade or

jam made with whole fruit, such as apricot, leave to cool for about 10 minutes before potting to prevent the fruit rising in the pots.

Pour or ladle the preserve into clean, dry, warm jars and fill to the top, to allow for shrinkage. After filling, put on well fitting waxed papers (wax side down on the jam).

Wipe the rims of the jars and cover the preserve with Cellophane circles or other suitable covering. Do this when the jam is still hot or wait until it is completely cold. Label each jar and store in a cool, dry place.

Hints for pressure cooking preserves
1. Use the pressure cooker without the trivet at medium (10 lb) pressure. Although it is possible to pre-cook the fruit at high (15 lb) pressure, a better colour and yield is obtained by cooking at medium (10 lb) pressure. Citrus fruits and vegetables for chutney may be cooked at high (15 lb) pressure.
2. Add water and cook fruit according to recipe.
3. Do not overfill the cooker. When the fruit or vegetables and water are in the cooker it should not be more than half full. This must allow for a full rolling boil once the sugar is added.
4. Allow the pressure to reduce slowly.
5. Once the sugar has been added, cook in the uncovered cooker. Never try to cook the preserves under pressure after the sugar has been added.
6. When adapting recipes for the pressure cooker, reduce the added liquid by half.

Guide to pressure cooking fruit for jams and jellies
pressure cooking time at medium (10 lb) pressure

Fruit	Jam	Jelly
Apples	5 minutes	7 minutes
Blackberries and apples	7 minutes	9 minutes
Blackcurrants	3–4 minutes	4 minutes
Damsons and other stone fruits	5 minutes	5 minutes
Gooseberries	3 minutes	3 minutes
Pears (hard cooking)	10 minutes	12 minutes
Quinces	10 minutes	12 minutes
Redcurrants	4 minutes	5 minutes
Citrus fruits at high (15 lb) pressure	20 minutes	25 minutes

Apple ginger jam

1·4 kg (3 lb) tart cooking apples
4 lemons
300 ml (½ pint) water
25 g (1 oz) ground ginger
1·4 kg (3 lb) sugar, warmed

Peel, core and slice the apples. Remove the lemon peel with a potato peeler and tie it in a piece of muslin with the peel and cores from the apples. Squeeze the juice from the lemon. Put the apples, lemon juice, water, ground ginger and the muslin bag in the pressure cooker. Put on the lid and bring to medium (10 lb) pressure. Cook for 5 minutes. Reduce pressure slowly.

Take out the muslin bag and squeeze all the juice into the cooker. Put the sugar in the cooker and stir until it is dissolved. Return the uncovered cooker to the heat and boil the jam rapidly, stirring all the time, until the setting point is reached. Remove the cooker from the heat. Allow the jam to settle for a few minutes, then pot and cover.
MAKES ABOUT 2.3 KG (5 LB).

Dried apricot jam

450 g (1 lb) dried apricots, washed
1·7 litres (3 pints) boiling water
juice and thinly peeled rind of 1 lemon
1·4 kg (3 lb) sugar, warmed

Cut the apricots into pieces, place them in the pressure cooker, pour on the boiling water and leave them to soak for 1 hour. Then add the lemon juice and peel in slivers. Put on the lid and bring to medium (10 lb) pressure. Cook for 15 minutes. Reduce pressure slowly. Discard the lemon peel. Put in the sugar and stir until it is dissolved. Return the uncovered cooker to the heat and boil the jam rapidly, stirring all the time, until the setting point is reached. Remove the cooker from the heat and allow the contents to settle, then pot and cover.
MAKES ABOUT 2.3 KG (5 LB).

Blackcurrant jam

900 g (2 lb) blackcurrants
400 ml (¾ pint) water
1·4 kg (3 lb) sugar, warmed

Remove the stalks and wash the fruit. Put the fruit in the cooker and add the water. Put on the lid and bring to medium (10 lb) pressure. Cook for 4 minutes. Reduce pressure slowly. Put in the sugar and stir until it is dissolved. Return the uncovered cooker to the heat and boil the jam rapidly, stirring all the time, until the setting point is reached. Remove the cooker from the heat, allow the contents to settle, then pot and cover.
MAKES ABOUT 2.3 KG (5 LB).

Plum jam

1·4 kg (3 lb) plums
300 ml (½ pint) water
1·4 kg (3 lb) sugar, warmed

Wash the plums, cut them in half and remove the stones. Crack some of the stones, remove the kernels and set them aside. Put the plums and water in the pressure cooker. Put on the lid and bring to medium (10 lb) pressure. Cook for 5 minutes. Reduce pressure slowly. Stir in the sugar until dissolved. Return the uncovered cooker to the heat and boil the contents rapidly, stirring all the time, until the setting point is reached. Stir in the blanched kernels. Remove the cooker from the heat and allow the jam to settle, then pot and cover.
MAKES ABOUT 2.3 KG (5 LB).

Quince jam

900 g (2 lb) quinces, prepared weight
400 ml (¾ pint) water
1·4 kg (3 lb) sugar, warmed

Peel, core and slice the quinces and weigh them. Put them in the pressure cooker with the water. Put on the lid and bring to medium (10 lb) pressure. Cook for 10 minutes. Reduce pressure slowly. Mash the quinces with a fork so that they are really pulpy. Then add the sugar and stir until it is dissolved. Return the uncovered cooker to the heat and boil the jam rapidly, stirring all the time, until the setting point is reached. Remove the cooker from the heat and allow the contents to settle, then pot and cover.
MAKES ABOUT 2.3 KG (5 LB).

Wash the blackberries and put them in the pressure cooker with the water and lemon juice. Put on the lid and bring to medium (10 lb) pressure. Cook for 8 minutes. Reduce pressure slowly. Strain the fruit through a jelly cloth or 2–3 thicknesses of muslin. Measure the extract and put it in the cooker to reheat. Meanwhile weigh the sugar, allowing 450 g (1 lb) sugar to each 500 ml (just under 1 pint) extract, and warm it. Remove the cooker from the heat, add the sugar and stir until it is dissolved. Return the uncovered cooker to the heat and boil the contents rapidly, stirring all the time, until setting point is reached. Remove the cooker from the heat and allow the contents to settle, then pot and cover.

MAKES 1·8–2·3 KG (4–5 LB).

Redcurrant jelly

1·4 kg (3 lb) redcurrants, stringed
300 ml (½ pint) water
sugar, warmed

Wash the fruit and put it in the pressure cooker with the water. Put on the lid and bring to medium (10 lb) pressure. Cook for 5 minutes. Reduce pressure slowly. Strain the fruit through a jelly cloth or 2–3 thicknesses of muslin. Measure the extract, return it to the cooker and reheat, uncovered. Remove the cooker from the heat. Weigh out the sugar, allowing 450 g (1 lb) to each 500 ml (just under 1 pint) of fruit extract, and warm it. Add the sugar to the cooker and stir until it is dissolved. Return the cooker to the heat and boil the jelly rapidly, stirring all the time, until setting point is reached. Remove the cooker from heat, allow the contents to settle, then pot and cover.

MAKES ABOUT 1·8–2·3 KG (4–5 LB).

Blackberry jelly

1·1 kg (2½ lb) under-ripe blackberries
300 ml (½ pint) water
juice of 2 lemons
sugar

Damson cheese

1·5 kg (3¾ lb) damsons
150 ml (¼ pint) water
sugar

Wash the fruit and remove the stalks. Put the fruit in the pressure cooker with the water. Put on the lid and bring to medium (10 lb) pressure. Cook for 5 minutes. Reduce pressure slowly. Sieve the fruit, discard the stones and weigh the pulp. Return to the cooker and heat gently, uncovered.

Meanwhile weigh the sugar, allowing 350 g (12 oz) to each 450 g (1 lb) fruit pulp, and warm it. Remove the cooker from the heat, add the sugar and stir until it is dissolved. Then return the uncovered cooker to the heat, and boil the contents rapidly, stirring all the time, until setting point is reached. Remove the cooker from the heat, allow the contents to settle, then pot and cover.

MAKES ABOUT 1·8 KG (4 LB).

Seville orange marmalade

900 g (2 lb) Seville oranges
2 small lemons
1·1 litres (2 pints) water
1·8 kg (4 lb) sugar, warmed

Wash and halve the oranges. Squeeze out the

juice and reserve all the juice and pips. Slice the peel thinly. Put the sliced peel, juice and water in the pressure cooker. Tie the pips and any soft pulp in a piece of muslin and add to the cooker. Put on the lid and bring to high (15 lb) pressure. Cook for 20 minutes. Reduce pressure slowly.

Allow the fruit to cool a little, then make sure that the peel is really soft by pressing it between the thumb and first finger. Take out the bag of pips and squeeze the juice from the bag into the cooker, then discard the bag. Add the sugar to the cooker and stir until it is dissolved. Return the uncovered cooker to the heat and boil the marmalade rapidly, stirring all the time, until setting point is reached. Remove the cooker from the heat and allow the marmalade to stand for about 10 minutes. Then stir it well, pot and cover. MAKES 2·7–3·2 KG (6–7 LB).

Orange marmalade
suitable for frozen fruit

450 g (1 lb) Seville oranges
600 ml (1 pint) water
1 lemon
900 g (2 lb) sugar, warmed

Put the whole washed fruit (do not thaw if frozen) in the pressure cooker with the water. Put on the lid and bring to high (15 lb) pressure. Cook for 20 minutes. Reduce pressure slowly. Remove the fruit.

Allow the fruit to cool a little, then make sure that the peel is really soft by pressing it between the thumb and forefinger. Then cut it up, using a knife and fork, and separate the pips at the same time. Put the pips in the liquid in the cooker, put on the lid and bring to high (15 lb) pressure. Cook for 5 minutes. Reduce pressure slowly. Strain the water and return it to the cooker. Put in the cooked peel and sugar and stir over low heat until the sugar is dissolved. Bring to the boil in uncovered cooker and boil rapidly, stirring all the time, until setting point is reached. Remove the cooker from the heat. Allow the contents to stand 10 minutes, then stir well, pot and cover. MAKES 1·4–1·8 KG (3–4 LB).

NB It is advisable to add one eighth extra weight

of Seville oranges when freezing for subsequent making in order to offset pectin loss.

Thick dark marmalade

900 g (2 lb) Seville oranges
2 small lemons
1 litre (1¾ pints) water
30 ml (2 level tbsp) treacle
1·8 kg (4 lb) sugar, warmed

Wash and halve the oranges. Squeeze out the juice and reserve the juice and pips. Cut the peel into thick slices. Tie the pips and any pulp in a piece of muslin. Put the peel, juice, water and muslin bag in the pressure cooker. Put on the lid and bring to high (15 lb) pressure. Cook for 20 minutes. Reduce pressure slowly.

Allow the fruit to cool a little, then make sure that the peel is really soft by pressing it between the thumb and forefinger. Add the treacle and sugar to the cooker and stir until it is dissolved. Return the uncovered cooker to the heat and boil the marmalade rapidly, stirring all the time, until setting point is reached. Remove the cooker from the heat and allow the contents to stand for about 10 minutes. Then stir well, pot and cover. MAKES 2·7–3·2 KG (6–7 LB).

Three fruit marmalade

Select fruit that weighs a total of 700 g (1½ lb).

2 lemons
1 large sweet orange
1 grapefruit
900 ml (1½ pints) water
1·4 kg (3 lb) sugar, warmed

Wash the fruit. Cut the lemons and orange in half, squeeze out the juice and remove the pips. Halve the grapefruit, squeeze out the juice; scoop out the pips and pulp and tie it with the other pips in a piece of muslin. Remove any thick pith from the grapefruit, then cut all the skins into thin slices. Put the fruit, muslin bag of pips, juice and water in the pressure cooker. Put on the lid and bring to high (15 lb) pressure. Cook for 20 minutes. Reduce the pressure slowly.

Allow the fruit to cool a little, then make sure

that the peel is really soft by squeezing it between the thumb and forefinger. Remove the bag of pips and squeeze the juice from the bag back into the cooker. Discard the bag. Add the sugar and stir until it is dissolved. Return the uncovered cooker to the heat and boil rapidly, stirring all the time, until setting point is reached. Remove the cooker from the heat and allow the contents to stand for about 10 minutes. Then stir the marmalade, pot and cover.

MAKES ABOUT 2·3 KG (5 LB).

Apple and tomato chutney

900 g (2 lb) apples, peeled, cored and sliced
450 g (1 lb) onions, skinned and sliced
450 g (1 lb) green tomatoes, sliced
2 cloves of garlic, skinned and chopped or crushed
20 ml (4 level tsp) salt
pinch of cayenne pepper
10 ml (2 level tsp) ground cinnamon
25 g (1 oz) ground ginger
300 ml (½ pint) malt vinegar
450 g (1 lb) demerara sugar
100 g (4 oz) sultanas

Put the prepared fruit and vegetables in the pressure cooker with the garlic, seasoning spices and vinegar. Put on the lid and bring to high (15 lb) pressure. Cook for 10 minutes. Reduce pressure slowly. Stir in the sugar and sultanas. Return the uncovered cooker to the heat and bring to the

boil, stirring, and cook rapidly to a thick consistency. Remove the cooker from the heat and allow the chutney to cool for about 10 minutes. Test for seasoning, then pot and cover. Keep the chutney for 2–3 months before using it.

MAKES ABOUT 900 G–1·4 KG (2–3 LB).

Green tomato chutney

700 g (1 ½ lb) green tomatoes, sliced
225 g (8 oz) onions, skinned
225 g (8 oz) apples, peeled and cored
100 g (4 oz) sultanas
5 ml (1 level tsp) salt
300 ml (½ pint) malt vinegar
20 ml (4 level tsp) ground ginger
pinch of cayenne pepper
5 ml (1 level tsp) dry mustard
100 g (4 oz) demerara sugar

Put the tomatoes, onions and apples through a coarse mincer. Then put them in the pressure cooker with the sultanas, salt, vinegar, spices and mustard. Put on the lid and cook for 10 minutes at high (15 lb) pressure. Reduce pressure slowly. Add the sugar and stir until it is dissolved. Return the uncovered cooker to the heat. Bring to the boil, stirring, and continue boiling until a thick consistency is reached. Remove the cooker from the heat and allow the chutney to cool for about 10 minutes. Test for seasoning, then pot and cover. Keep the chutney for 2 months before using.

MAKES ABOUT 900 G–1·4 KG (2–3 LB).

Indian chutney

This is a hot chutney, which is very good with curry. The spices may be adjusted to taste.

225 g (8 oz) dried apricots, cut into pieces
225 g (8 oz) cooking apples, peeled, cored and sliced
225 g (8 oz) onions, skinned and sliced
2 cloves of garlic, skinned and crushed
20 ml (4 level tsp) salt
300 ml (½ pint) malt vinegar
30 ml (2 level tbsp) ground ginger
1·25 ml (¼ level tsp) cayenne pepper
2·5 ml (½ level tsp) cummin powder
450 g (1 lb) soft brown sugar
225 g (8 oz) stoned or seedless raisins, chopped

Pour about 600 ml (1 pint) boiling water on to the apricots and leave to soak for at least 1 hour. Drain off remaining water and put the apricots in the pressure cooker with the apples, onions, garlic, salt, vinegar and spices. Put on the lid and bring to high (15 lb) pressure. Cook for 15 minutes. Reduce pressure slowly. Add the sugar and raisins and stir until the sugar is dissolved. Return the uncovered cooker to the heat and bring to the boil, stirring. Boil the chutney until a thick consistency is reached. Remove the cooker from the heat and allow the contents to cool for about 10 minutes, then pot and cover.

MAKES ABOUT 1·4–1·8 KG (3–4 LB).

Rhubarb chutney

1·1 kg (2 ½ lb) coarse rhubarb
225 g (8 oz) onions, skinned and minced
15 ml (1 level tbsp) ground ginger
15 ml (1 level tbsp) salt
25 g (1 oz) pickling spice, tied in a piece of muslin
300 ml (½ pint) vinegar
450 g (1 lb) soft brown sugar
100 g (4 oz) sultanas

Wash the rhubarb and cut it into 5-cm (2-in) lengths. Put the rhubarb in the pressure cooker with the onions, ginger, salt, the bag of pickling spice and the vinegar. Put on the lid and bring to high (15 lb) pressure. Cook for 10 minutes. Reduce pressure slowly. Add the sugar and sultanas and stir until the sugar is dissolved. Discard the bag of spice. Return the uncovered cooker to the heat and bring to the boil, stirring. Boil the chutney until a thick consistency is reached. Remove the cooker from the heat and allow the contents to cool for about 10 minutes, then pot and cover. Leave the chutney to mature for at least 3 months before using.

MAKES ABOUT 1·4 KG (3 LB).

GENERAL GUIDE TO BOTTLING FRUIT IN A PRESSURE COOKER

Preparation of jars

Wash the special bottling jars thoroughly and rinse in clean, hot water. Discard any jars with cracks or chips. Inspect glass lids for defects. Some metal covers can always be re-used, provided the lacquer inside is intact and the shape is retained.

Preparation of fruit

Wash and prepare the fruit according to type (see chart) and discard any damaged or overripe fruit. Sort fruit so that each jar contains fruit of uniform size. Cut large fruits into equal sized pieces. Fruit which discolours when exposed to the air (such as apples and pears) should be immersed in a light brine (see page 125) until required. Rinse the fruit just before packing it in the jars.

Packing the fruit in jars

Pack the fruit neatly in the jars so that there are few air spaces. Fill to the shoulder of the jar.

It is best to bottle fruit in sugar syrup as it helps to mature the flavour. The syrup can be light or heavy (see page 125). After filling the warm jars with fruit, pour the boiling syrup slowly over the fruit and fill to within 2·5 cm (1 in) of the top. Tap the jars once or twice to release any air bubbles.

Fit the tops on to the jars, according to the type. Screw rings should always be screwed on tightly, then released half a turn to allow room for expansion.

Sterilising fruit in the pressure cooker

Put the trivet in the pressure cooker and pour in at least 1·1 litres (2 pints) water and bring to the boil.

Place the filled jars on the trivet, leaving a little space around each one. Put on the lid without the weight and allow the steam to escape as a steady flow before putting on the weight. Then bring the cooker to low (5 lb) pressure quickly – it should not take longer than 5 minutes. Sterilise the fruit for the required time, as given in the chart.

Turn off the heat and allow the pressure to reduce slowly, for at least 10 minutes. Then remove the lid, take out the jars of fruit and stand them on a wooden surface. Tighten the screw caps if used. Leave to cool.

Storing

The following day, test the seal. To do this, remove the screw ring or metal clip and lift each jar by the lid. It should not move. If the lid does move, use the fruit immediately and check the jar, lid and screw ring or clip for faults before using them again.

Wipe the bottles and grease the rings, if used, to prevent rusting (Vaseline is useful for this).

Label the jars and put them in a cool dark place to store.

Sterilising times for bottled fruit in syrup

As timing is critical, a minute 'pinger' timer is very useful for sterilising.

Fruit	Preparation	Sterilising time in pressure cooker at low (5 lb) pressure
Apples	Peel, core and slice. During preparation, keep in a brine solution (see page 125). Rinse quickly in cold water before packing in jars.	1 minute
Apricots	Remove stalks, wash fruit. Leave whole or halve and stone. Crack some of the stones and remove kernels to include with the fruit. Pack quickly to prevent browning.	1 minute
Blackberries	Pick over, remove damaged fruit. Wash carefully. Remove stalks.	1 minute
Blackcurrants	String, pick over and wash.	1 minute
Cherries	Remove stalks and wash. Remove stones, if wished.	1 minute
Damsons	Remove stems and wash fruit.	1 minute
Figs	Remove stems; peel if wished. Add 2·5 ml (½ level tsp) citric acid to each 600 ml (1 pint) syrup, to give acidity and ensure good keeping. Pack with an equal amount of syrup.	5 minutes
Gooseberries	Top, tail and wash. To prevent shrivelling if bottled in syrup, prick the skins.	1 minute
Grapefruit	Peel, remove pith, divide into segments and remove membrane.	1 minute
Greengages	Remove stalks and wash.	1 minute
Loganberries	Remove hulls and pick over. Avoid washing if possible.	1 minute
Nectarines	Wash and dice.	1 minute
Peaches	Scald and skin, halve and stone.	1 minute

Fruit	Preparation	Sterilising time in pressure cooker at low (5 lb) pressure
Pears	Peel, core and halve. During preparation, keep in water containing 10 ml (2 level tsp) salt and 7·5 ml (1½ level tsp) citric acid per 1·1 litre (2 pints). Rinse quickly in cold water before packing.	5 minutes
Plums	Wash, remove stalks. Leave whole or halve and stone. Crack some of the stones and include kernels.	1 minute
Raspberries	Remove hulls and, pick over. Avoid washing if possible.	1 minute
Redcurrants	String and wash.	1 minute
Rhubarb	Wash, trim and cut into 5-cm (2-in) lengths.	1 minute
Tomatoes	Scald, skin and halve. Fill jars with boiling brine (see below).	5 minutes

Sugar syrup
50–100 g (2–4 oz) sugar, for light syrup
225 g (8 oz) sugar, for heavy syrup
600 ml (1 pint) water

Dissolve the sugar in the water over very low heat. When sugar is completely dissolved, bring to the boil. Boil for 2–3 minutes.

Brine
Add 15 ml (1 level tbsp) salt to 1 litre (1¾ pints) water. Bring brine to the boil.

INDEX